FUN CITY
An Ethnographic Study of a Retirement Community

FUN CITY

An Ethnographic Study of a Retirement Community

By

JERRY JACOBS
Syracuse University

Waveland Press, Inc.
Prospect Heights, Illinois

For information about this book, write or call:

Waveland Press, Inc.
P.O. Box 400
Prospect Heights, Illinois 60070
(312) 634-0081

Foreword

About the Author

Jerry Jacobs is an Associate Professor of Sociology at Syracuse University and is affiliated with the Sociology Department and the All University Gerontology Center where he is currently directing a study of a campus-based retirement setting. He was formerly with the University of California at Riverside and San Francisco and is the author of numerous articles and books.

He has edited *Getting By: Illustrations of Marginal Living* (Little, Brown & Co., 1972), and written *The Search for Help: A Study of the Retarded Child in the Community* (Brunner/Mazel, 1969), and *Adolescent Suicide* (John Wiley & Sons, 1971).

About the Book

Fun City is an activity-centered as well as an age-centered planned community in a warm valley of the West. It boasts 92 clubs and organizations to help make it possible for the approximately 5,600 inhabitants to lead an active life. Dr. Jacobs studies this community to find out whether, indeed, the Fun City way of life is an active one and to relate what he finds to the larger framework of gerontological theory. He feels that ethnographies of retirement communities and of age-centered groups are necessary for the development of meaningful theoretical models.

There can be no denying the significance of such studies as this book represents. There has been a 538 percent increase in the retirement-age population in the United States since 1900. Retirement communities of the type described in this case study are one answer to the problem of what to do with one's advanced years. It is well to remember, however, that Fun City is an alternative for only the relatively affluent.

The situation this case study analyzes is something that readers of all ages should be interested in, for the majority of people—even in their teens and 20's, barring some great catastrophe—will someday face retirement. What to do with one's waning years is not, however, a problem of equal magnitude in all human societies. In many it is a period of special influence and prestige, particularly in ceremonial or sacred matters, and sometimes in the political arena. In some cultures it is a time to be ignored. In very few human cultures is it a time for segregation, as it is increasingly in ours. Handling the problems of an elderly population by segregation reflects the nomadic and fragmented character of American social and particularly familial life. Segregation, coupled with a marked increase in the population being segregated, creates social and psychological problems of its own. Many of these problems become abundantly clear in Dr. Jacobs' description of Fun City.

However segregated this or any other community for the elderly retired may be, it is well to remember that Fun City is not qualitatively different from the rest of American middle class society. Its wide streets, spaced houses with separate lawns, and lack of transportation facilities, except for the private automobile, are direct extensions of middle class suburban communities throughout the United States, and it is not merely the material structures and use of space that are the same. The people inside the houses are separated from each other and lonely, like the people in ordinary suburban communities, but the weakness of old age makes some of them even lonelier.

GEORGE AND LOUISE SPINDLER

Contents

1/Fun City: An overview

A DESCRIPTION OF THE TOWN

Fun City, "an active way of life," is nestled in a warm valley, about ninety miles southeast of a large metropolitan area, where the prevailing winds are such as to keep it relatively free from smog. The community itself is situated adjacent to a major state artery and is comprised of 5700 persons (6500 if we accept the realtor's estimate) over the age of fifty. The average resident is sixty-three years old.

The city itself is organized around wide, well-kept streets that are remarkable in several ways: (1) they are all about the width of a four-lane highway; (2) there are no cars parked in the streets; (3) there are few cars driven on them; (4) they are all immaculately clean—no cigarette butts, gum wrappers, toothpicks, match sticks, bent beer cans, broken bottles, animal excrements, or less seemly items (the usual tell-tale signs of urban or rural life) are to be found in the streets of Fun City; (5) they are all lined on both sides with sidewalks that no one walks on; and (6) all of the city's streets and sidewalks can be observed at any time of the day or night in the same state of eerie desolation.

These streets are lined with row after row of well-kept tract homes, varying in price from $19,000 to $50,000. The houses exhibit many of the same characteristics as the streets. They are immaculately kept inside and out. All have white gravel or shingle roofs that, from a distance, accentuate Fun City's gray-on-gray architecture. Most have front lawns of crushed rock frequently stained green, and, perhaps, one or more live or plastic bushes to enhance the landscaping decor.

From the street the homes show no signs of life. The inhabitants themselves are rarely, if ever, seen walking the sidewalks, sitting outside their homes, tending the yard, or making repairs. The only sign of habitation is the row after row of large, late-model American cars stationed in the carports. If viewed from a distance, Fun City appears to be a cross between a suburban tract community being readied for habitation and a large, cleverly camouflaged used car lot.

Three other Fun City facilities are worthy of note. Now under construction are a series of "garden apartments' which will provide the residents with maid service and a central eating area. When completed these apartments will offer an intermediate setting for residents, somewhere between the home owners and apartment dwellers (those who are able to care for themselves) and those who can no longer

1

Fun City.

care for themselves and who reside in the adjacent nursing home. With the completion of these apartments a full range of living accommodations will be available to the resident to meet his every need, from early retirement to death. While the garden apartments are being built on the west side of town along a main thoroughfare, the Fun City ambulance service, nursing home, and mortuary, arranged in that order, are located on the outskirts of town and out of sight.

The city's development was undertaken about ten years ago as a commercial venture designed to meet the growing needs of retirement age persons (the number of persons in this age group has increased 538 percent since the turn of the century). It was envisaged as an activities-centered planned community, designed to help overcome some of the shock one was likely to experience upon being subject to the abrupt transition from a work to a leisure life style. In this regard there are three sectors of town that partially succeed in fulfilling this goal: the Town Hall–Activities Center area, the Civic Hall–Golf Club area, and the Shopping Center area. This entire complex is encompassed in a territory of about six square blocks. Leave this locale and there is only the unreal feeling of desolation and isolation I have described above.

Not only are the residents isolated from the Activities Center; the entire city is isolated from other urban life. For example, there is no industry in or about the town. Fun City is not a suburb of a large metropolitan area. Because of its isolation and other characteristics, Fun City has much in common with other "total-institutional" settings. It is geographically isolated, it is open only to a restricted membership, and it has effectively isolated an "undesirable element"

Law and order in the streets.

from the greater community. It has also managed to impose upon the residents a series of contractual and institutional constraints that have effectively severed most of them from the means of overcoming their discontents. However, one alternative open to the residents that is not usually found in such settings is their right to leave Fun City and seek its promise elsewhere. Many have taken this option.

In all fairness, the notion of "total institution" in the above context is of only marginal utility. Allowing for the geographic isolation of Fun City, which at least in part is due to the scarcity of large tracts of cheap land and/or the prevalent notion that the isolation of the aged is in their best interest, the author does not mean to imply that its planners and developers intended to isolate the residents from each other. This isolation is in large part self-imposed. The reason for this lack of social interaction, notwithstanding the developers' intentions, will be discussed at a later point in greater detail.

LOCAL GOVERNMENT

Fun City is peculiar in yet another regard. It has no fire department, police department, or major medical facilities of its own. Fun City is an unincorporated town. It has no mayor or usual governmental apparatus. The formal features of Fun City's government (or lack of it) and its implications for different segments of the citizenry will be considered in greater detail later. It is enough at this point

"Low maintenance" yards.

to note that one of the major reasons residents give for coming to Fun City is security. That an aging population of white middle class property owners, many of them in poor health, seek "security" in an isolated social environment which has no police department, fire department, or major health facilities is an enigma that will receive our further attention in Chapter 4.

THE ACTIVITY CENTER

The Activity Center's facilities are contained within an area of about two square blocks. Its hub is the Town Hall. This is a large, air-conditioned auditorium that holds an estimated 300 people. Apart from the main hall itself, there are three smaller rooms: the ladies' clubroom, the men's clubroom, and, adjacent to the men's clubroom, a tiny room used by the maintenance personnel. The main hall in Town Hall is usually reserved for large-scale social functions. For example, the following clubs and events use the main hall: the Camera Club, orchestra practice, Molly's Corner (a once-a-week, two-hour, social get-together with music, dance, and refreshments), the Garden Club, band practice, lawn-bowling luncheon, public speakers, or any other gathering likely to draw a large crowd.

The men's clubroom (about the size of the women's clubroom, perhaps 15 by 20 feet) is used primarily for card games. Several card tables accommodating four players each are almost always in use. The men's clubroom is also used by the American Legion, or for lectures to small groups on practical topics, such as income tax preparation or health or auto insurance, or for games less popular than cards, such as chess or checkers.

Molly's Corner.

The ladies' clubroom is used for small group activities or intimate gatherings. For example, language classes, Religious Science study groups, typing classes, executive dinner club meetings, Scrabble players, and gatherings of the Fun City TOPS (Take Off Pounds) Club, meet here.

Opposite Town Hall, and connected to it by an overhang, is another large air-conditioned hall and activity complex—North Town Hall. This is the staging area for such weekly or monthly events as the Square Dance Club, physical fitness classes, "Defensive Driving" class, Glee Club practice, ballroom dancing, Christian Science Society meetings, Bicycle Club get-togethers, and any other public or organizational function requiring a lot of space or likely to draw a large crowd.

Behind Town Hall is a large concrete patio area and semicircular forum with low, backless benches. Adjacent to this is a brick fenced-in area that encloses a sheltered patio complete with tables, chairs, chaises longues, and two large pools, one larger than the other, separated by a brick wall. Both pools are frequently empty, even on warm days, and it is rare to find more than three or four people in the pool at once. Indoors is a third, much smaller, heated therapeutic whirlpool bath. Adjacent to the sheltered pool and patio area is the Arts and Crafts area. This is a series of rooms contained in a low, well-kept brick building, organized around a courtyard. The Arts and Crafts area contains an art classroom, photo lab, sewing room, trophy room (a kind of lounge area), a ceramics club, wood-working shop, and lapidary and jewelry shop.

Finally, there is the Civic Hall (and golf club area) that is a smaller and less pretentious activity center than Town Hall or North Town Hall and is used for large-scale game attractions, such as the bridge club, pinochle club, canasta club, or for Bible and travel club meetings.

THE SHOPPING CENTER

While most formal interactions take place around the planned activities staged within the Activity Center, informal interactions are frequently initiated within the shopping center. This setting is comprised of thirty-nine small businesses grouped in a rectangle. Each establishment is protected by an overhang that pro-vides both shop and shopper with protection from the sun. A list of shopping center establishments and a diagram noting their position and relative size is given on the following page. A description of the residents' activities within the Shopping Center and the kinds of informal interactions that ensue will be considered in detail in Chapter 2.

SOMETHING FOR EVERYONE?

If the reader has the impression from the descriptions of the Town Hall-Activi-ties Center and the Civic Hall-Golf Club area that there are a great many planned activities and clubs in Fun City, he is correct. The *Fun City News*, a weekly community newspaper, lists the week's events by date and time of day. A typical week's calendar lists about 150 separate social events, most of which are con-

Swim time.

FUN CITY SHOPPING CENTER

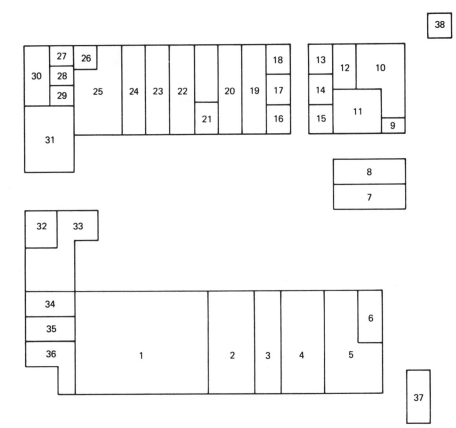

1. Supermarket
2. Variety Store
3. Drug Store
4. Hardware Store
5. Furniture and Carpet Store
6. Department of Building and Safety
7. Auto Parts and Bike Store
8. Beauty Shop
9. Travel Agent
10. Snack Shop
11. County Library
12. Chiropractor
13. Attorney
14. Vacant
15. Christian Science Reading Room
16. Snack Shop Office
17. Insurance Agent
18. *Fun City News*
19. Electrical Appliance Store
20. Coffee Shop
21. Jewelry Store
22. Health Food Store
23. Billiards Parlor
24. Transfer and Storage
25. General Office of Fun City Realty
26. Attorney
27. Letter Shop
28. Communications
29. Laundry
30. Savings and Loan
31. Liquor Store
32. Insurance Agent
33. Cleaning Store
34. Self-service Laundry
35. Barber Shop
36. Women's Wear
37. Nursery
38. Post Office

The Shopping Center.

ducted within the activity center. Approximately 65 of these are morning activities, 60 afternoon, and about 25 evening. Fun City boasts a total of 92 different clubs and organizations. For a population of approximately 6000 persons, this would certainly seem to provide something for everyone.

Who participates in these activities? How many members do these organizations have? How many active members? And finally, how many of Fun City's 6000 residents participate in "an active way of life"? A head count at different times of the day and on different days of the week undertaken early in the study revealed how few of Fun City's residents participate in the planned activities. There are never more than between two and three hundred—frequently fewer than that—residents participating in the planned activities provided by the .Town Hall–Activities Center and the Civic Hall–Golf Club area on any one day, even when we include the evening activities. More telling is the fact that these participants are almost always the same persons. A generous estimate would be that there are another three to four hundred persons to be found in or about the Shopping Center area. In brief, one might on a busy, warm, clear day account for between five and eight hundred persons within the boundaries of Fun City. The question arises, in light of previous description of the streets and residences, where the other five thousand residents are and what this *invisible majority* is doing.

I will lead into an answer to this question by discussing the activities of the *visible minority*. The latter is comprised of two groups, those participating in the *planned activities* that are a part of the Town Hall–Activities Center–Golf Club complex, and those shoppers and casual socializers participating in the *informal activities* provided by and located within the Shopping Center.

2 / The visible minority:
An active way of life

THE SHOPPING CENTER: STAGING AREA FOR INFORMAL INTERACTIONS

The Shopping Center is probably Fun City's most popular staging area for informal forms of interaction. Notwithstanding this fact, many of the residents are there for reasons other than, or in addition to, their search for companionship. The following is a description of the Center's businesses and their effects upon the residents' social life.

First and foremost is the supermarket, which, until recently, had a monopoly on food distribution services in Fun City. This monopoly was a sore spot for the residents, who claimed that the service given, the choice of food, and its costs were not competitive with markets in nearby towns. This problem has been alleviated if not resolved with the recent opening of a second supermarket. The greatest number of cars is always parked in the vicinity of the markets, which also contain by far the greatest number of shoppers. The two coffee shops located at the opposite side of the Shopping Center are next in popularity (see diagram of the center in Chapter 1). These four food-related businesses not only consistently draw the greatest number of residents, but also provide an important staging area for initiating casual and more intense forms of social interactions among Fun City shoppers.

THE SHOPS

Before considering who uses these facilities and how they do so, I would like to discuss briefly some of the other businesses that operate within the Shopping Center, in order to put the four major ones into perspective (see the complete list of businesses noted in Chapter 1). Business in the Shopping Center is usually conducted on a Monday-through-Saturday, 8:00 A.M. to 5:30 P.M., basis. Nearly all activity in the Shopping Center ceases at about 6:00 P.M. From that point on, one of the few signs of life emanates from the Town Hall–Activity Center area or from the only combination restaurant, cocktail lounge, coffee shop, and motel in town, The Royal Inn, located directly across the street from the Shopping Center. The remainder of the city, its immaculate residences, streets, and sidewalks, appears completely deserted. There is only the yellow flicker of lamp lights,

A day at the beauty parlor.

mixed with eerie white lights of TV screens shimmering through the drawn drapes, to indicate the presence of Fun City's inhabitants.

How do these small businesses fare? Apart from the brisk trade at the two coffee shops and supermarkets, one gets the impression that performance is spotty, and business could be better. While some businesses may have as many as a dozen persons shopping on occasion, others are almost always empty. The variety store, drug store, beauty shop, laundromat, and barber shop seem to do comparatively well, while business at the appliance store, furniture store, and ladies' wear shop is consistently slow. Although the most active stores, economically and socially, are the four food-related ones, others also offer fertile interactional settings. This is true not only because of their relatively strong patronage, but because of their physical settings. Barber shops, beauty shops, and self-service laundries have the following features in common: (1) patrons spend relatively long periods of time in each other's company; (2) this time is spent in close proximity to others; (3) one has nothing to do in these situations—one looks for ways to "pass time"; (4) these establishments do a predictable "repeat business" so that the owners and/or patrons come to know one another; (5) in such social settings, casual interactions in the form of "small talk" are both acceptable and expected. The variety store and supermarkets also allow for unhurried browsing by Fun City's residents, some of whom know or at least recognize one another. They provide numerous (if not lengthy) encounters among residents who might otherwise have little or no social contact with one another. The coffee shops, although they exhibit many of the above features, offer a setting and form of interaction that are qualitatively

A Fun City supermarket.

different and contribute to more meaningful forms of interaction over longer periods of time.

The Coffee Shops

The coffee shop, apart from offering a common meeting ground for Fun City residents during meal hours, provides a setting for more intense forms of interactions than are characteristic of supermarket, drug-store, or variety-store encounters. Coffee-shop interactions are more like those found in the beauty shop. This evaluation is based upon two facts. First, the coffee and beauty shops are meeting places for persons who already know one another. Women frequently schedule beauty-shop appointments at the same time every week, which means that patrons who are not formally acquainted at the outset will be likely to make each other's acquaintance in the course of time. The same is true of the coffee shop, where many patrons congregate at the same time of the day, every day of the week. It is clear that the two coffee shops are common meeting grounds for old friends. Another aspect of the coffee- and beauty-shop setting is that, unlike the market or variety store, people routinely spend long periods of time in each other's presence, a condition that encourages the initiation of more meaningful forms of interaction.

You may remember that there are two coffee shops in the Shopping Center, # 10 and # 20 on the diagram given in Chapter 1. The shops, although only a few yards apart, have different atmospheres, ecologies, and patronages, and foster different kinds of interactions. There are many reasons for this. For example, both have booths and a counter, but different seating arrangements. The counter at the corner shop accommodates fewer persons, is situated in a straight line, and faces the wall, while the counter in the second shop (# 20) is in the center of the store and in the form of a U. It seats a greater number of persons, all of whom can look at each other. Add to this the fact that the proprietress-waitress is stationed within this centrally located U as a kind of down-home roving ambassador-at-large while keeping up a lively patter with the elderly patrons (and steady customers), and we have the makings of a successful business enterprise and informal staging area for relatively strong and extended forms of interactions. Not only does the other eatery (# 10) not have the proper ecology for this counter-entered society, but it does not have a proprietor capable of mingling with the customers and ensuring the interaction that such an organizational arrangement promises. The atmosphere of the corner shop then may be characterized as "formal," while that of the other shop is "easy." The food and price lists of the two are comparable.

Another feature of the coffee shops that helps to account for the relative extent of meaningful interaction is the design and location of the booths. Many of the booths in the corner shop are located side by side in the center of the shop, while the others are placed around them in a U. None of the booths is separated by partitions. This seating arrangement affords the corner-shop customers little privacy. The other shop overcomes this handicap by placing its booths back to back, so that persons in one booth cannot easily see or hear what transpires in another. Then too, the booths are situated in a U formation which is separated by the U-shaped counter located in the center of the shop. This distribution effectively isolates the customers in one booth from those in another and helps contribute a feeling of privacy. The net result is a more open and animated conversation among booth and counter customers.

The Library

Also located within the shopping center is the county-operated Fun City library. It is staffed by the librarian and a helper (both Fun City residents) and a second part-time helper, a young college girl. The library is open Monday and Wednesday from 10:00 A.M. to 5:00 P.M., Tuesday and Thursday from 1:00 P.M. to 8:00 P.M., and Saturday from 10:00 A.M. to 2:00 P.M. Nearly all of the 3118 library cards issued have gone to Fun City residents. A few were issued to residents in neighboring small towns, mobile home sites, or outlying districts in which library facilities are unavailable. The library boasts a collection of about 7000 volumes and has a circulation of about 4000 books and periodicals a month. In describing the kinds of literature most popular among Fun City residents the librarian summed it up this way: "Mostly mysteries, 'escape literature,' you know —things to go to sleep by."

The Stock Exchange

A final informal socializing center for Fun City residents within the Shopping Center complex is the stock exchange room of one of the two banks flanking the

The "counter-centered" coffee shop.

Shopping Center proper. Some of Fun City's more prosperous citizens congregate at the stock exchange room (usually during the morning hours) to discuss the stock market and other news of the day. For many, this activity comprises an important part of their daily routine.

An Overview

In general, shopping in Fun City is disappointing. As we will see later, getting to and from the shopping center is a problem. Many residents are no longer able to drive, and Fun City has no public transportation. Because of infirmities and the hot weather, only those who live within a few blocks of the shopping center are able to walk there. This excludes many from easy access, since the center is not located in the geographical center of town but on the periphery. Quite apart from the problem of getting to and from, the shopping itself leaves much to be desired. One Fun City resident put it this way:

> The shopping is very disheartening here. That's one of the most frustrating things. And I think that's why Mission X [another retirement community] grew with such leaps and bounds as they did because women like it because it was near the shopping centers. You see, it gave them a place to go shopping and that always makes for a lot of contentment, believe me, to be able to get to the stores, [and] see things ... That's one of women's biggest gripes.

Fun City residents usually do their major shopping during their one-day "outings" to neighboring towns. Many retired military personnel shop at the post exchange at a nearby military base, where shopping is not only more convenient, but also much less expensive. Shopping as something to do, and the shopping center as a place to go (either to buy merchandise or meet people) plays an important part in the life of Fun City residents. Had these facilities been expanded, the prices competitive, and the shopping center itself more conveniently located (or more readily available through free or inexpensive public transportation) it could better serve as a center for promoting meaningful informal social activities, thereby contributing a great deal to residents' morale.

Keeping in mind the forms and extent of informal interactions found within the shopping center, let us now consider in greater detail those found in the more formal settings of the Activity Center–Town Hall area.

THE ACTIVITY CENTER: STAGING AREA FOR FORMAL INTERACTIONS

As noted earlier, approximately 500 of Fun City's 6000 residents participate in the planned activities held within the Activity Center–Town Hall area. With this in mind, four basic questions present themselves: (1) How many residents belong to Fun City's clubs and organizations? (2) How many of these are active members? (3) How many are nonmembers? (4) How do these three categories of persons spend their leisure time?

A look at the *"Fun City Guide: An Organizational Guide in Alphabetical Order*—listing all fraternal, business, social, civic, religious, and service groups in Fun City" is revealing. Excluding the business and religious listings and considering all of the others as potential sources of social- and leisure-time activity, there are 92 clubs and organizations available to Fun City residents.[1] Let us consider first some of the larger clubs and their memberships.

MAJOR HOBBY CLUBS

The largest hobby club is the Arts and Crafts Club, which lists 198 members and meets at 7:30 P.M. on the third Friday of each month (except during July and August) in the Town Hall auditorium. Board meetings are held at 1:30 P.M. on the second Thursday of each month in the women's club room. The arts and crafts facilities that were outlined earlier are open to members daily from 10:00 to 12:00 and from 1:00 to 3:00. They include an art class, sewing club, photo lab, ceramics shop, wood shop, and lapidary and jewelry shop. In all cases, craft teachers are Fun City resident volunteers.

The distribution of membership by sex in these clubs is as follows: the art, sewing, and ceramic classes are attended exclusively by women; the wood shop and the lapidary (jewelry) shop exclusively by men; and the photo lab (primarily Camera Club members) by both sexes, with a preponderance of men. On a typical day, the distribution of the 198 members is roughly as follows: ceramics, 4–10 members; wood shop, 2–6; lapidary and jewelry shop, 2–6; art class, 0–6; sewing class, 0–8. The photo lab is fronted by a solid door so that it is impossible to know

---

[1] The social role of the Church will be considered separately.

from the outside when it is in use. However, I have on only two or three occasions seen anyone entering or leaving the photo lab. In fact, it is unusual to see more than 20 to 30 persons using the arts and crafts facilities on any one day. There are many days when there are fewer than a dozen. Furthermore, it seems that those who use the facilities are almost always the same persons. What of the other members of the Arts and Crafts Club? Although I am unable to give an accurate accounting of their activities, one thing is certain: Their activities do not include active participation in arts and crafts.

The Camera Club

Another club with a relatively large membership is the Camera Club, which boasts 141 members. As I have noted, the photo lab seems to be in little demand. At a meeting of the Camera Club I attended, on the occasion of a slide exhibit and judging for "best picture" awards (something of an event in Fun City's camera world), there were approximately 40 persons present (equally divided between men and women). A very formal air prevailed throughout the meeting, and the general posture was one of polite attention to speakers but very little interaction among club members. The following transcribed excerpt will help to convey some flavor of the meeting to the reader.

Mary: . . . and on May twenty-seventh Mary and Bruce B. from out of town will be here and they are members of the Intershow Masters. They are excellent photographers and their programs are always perfectly beautiful, beautifully staged, and just excellent in every detail. And their title this time is "The South American Odyssey," and the highlight of that particular program is their trip to the lost city of Montepichu. Those of you who have been down there will see some really beautiful slides of the lost city in this program. And on

The Ladies' Art Club.

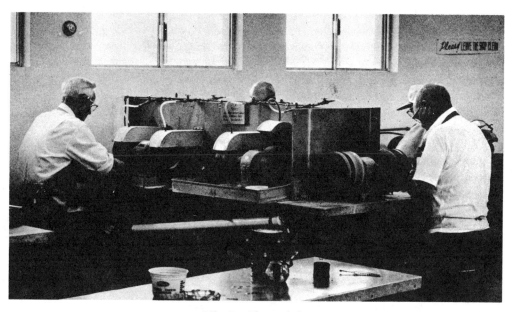

The Lapidary Club.

June twenty-fourth, Joan and Chuck C. from out of town will be here with their wonderful program . . . I'm using a lot of superlatives . . . to see three terrific programs in a row . . . their beautiful program—"Colonies in Paradise." They include South Sea Islands and they took three trips back into the remote areas where most of the tourists never set foot, and they put all these new slides to South Sea Island music, so you know that's going to be just great. And then on July twenty-second . . . hometown talent, and Dave D. is this year going to handle that for us, so be sure to give your slides to me by June first and I'll turn them over to Dave. Thank you. (Applause)

Dave: Thank you, Mary. Mary has used a lot of superlatives . . . too loud or not loud enough? How's that? That better, can everybody hear me? [problem with the microphone.] We do have some marvelous programs coming up. We have the best programs that have ever been put together by a camera club, so you've got a lot of good things to look forward to. So, Joyce, if you can give me a hand, we have the present beauty tonight, pass out a few ribbons, so if the following people would come up here and line themselves around here . . . Harry R. . . . Harry isn't here tonight. *Mary C.* . . . I know she's not here. Gladys D. . . . she's not here. Oh, is she here? I didn't see her. Come on up here Gladys. . . . Frank D. . . . Frank's not here? . . . John S. . . . I know he's here tonight. I think I saw John. . . . Emily B. . . . Ben R. and Ray J. is not here. Now, Joyce. . . . we just got a lot of winners who unfortunately can't be here tonight. Harry H., who is not here, is third place in Class A, "Virgin Wool," Mary J. . . . could not be here tonight either. . . . Gladys, first place, Class A. . . . now if you will present this to Cecil I., third place . . . will you please give that to me? Thank you so much. (Applause) Now Joyce . . . second place, Class A, "Colored Glass," Joyce, may I present that to you. (Applause) Class A, Frank B., first place . . . . John S., third place in Black and White . . . . Emily J., second place in Black and White . . . . Frank B., first place in Black and White. Congratulations, Frank. . . . Then a fellow by the name of Ben D., third place, Class AA . . . . then another fellow . . .

Card Clubs

While many of the large membership clubs that purportedly contribute to "an active way of lire" have very little real participation, some large hobby clubs that contribute to a passive way of life have very active memberships. These are primarily card clubs. For example, there is the Bridge Club (Party Contract), 650 members; Bridge Club (Duplicate), 110 members; Canasta Club, 100 members; Pinochle Club (Monday night), 125 members; and Pinochle Club (Wednesday night), 70 members. Card games (either the small games in the men's club room or the larger games in Civic Hall) are always well attended. In addition, many card club members and nonmembers who do not attend the club's organized programs meet in each other's homes on a regular basis in groups of four to eight for an afternoon or evening of cards. Card games as a planned formal activity or informal get-together constitute a means of spending a good part of one's leisure time (in the company of others) for a large proportion of Fun City's residents.

Minor Hobby Clubs

In addition to the major hobby clubs I have described, there are a number of minor hobby clubs, such as the Chess and Checkers Club, 31 members; Coin Club, 30 members; Stamp Club, 38 members; Creative Writing Club, 20 members; and the Scrabble Club, 20 members. These activities are usually poorly attended —for example in the course of numerous trips to Fun City I have only once seen a chess game in progress. In general, one must conclude that intellectual pursuits, such as creative writing, chess, and stamp collecting have at best a small following among Fun City residents.

MAJOR SPORTS CLUBS

There are, of course, some clubs whose activities contribute to an active way of life that have both a large and an active membership. The five major ones are the Golf, Shuffleboard, Lawn Bowls, Square Dance, and Bicycle Clubs.

The Golf Club

Perhaps the most active of the five is the Golf Club. Membership in the Golf Club was noted in the *Guide* as follows: Golf Association (Men's), 312 members; Golf Association (Women's), 104 members; Golf Association (Women's) The Niners, 53 members; Golf Association (Men's) North Course, 107 members; Golf Association (Women's) North Course, 68 members.

This adds up to a grand total of 644 Fun City residents who are members of one of a series of golfing clubs. (There is little, if any, overlap in the membership.) How many persons is one likely to find on the fairway on a good day? While estimates are based only upon those sections of the course visible from Fun City's streets there are probably not more than 50 to 75 persons using the fairways on

The Ladies' Card Club.

any one day.[2] This estimate was supported by other indicators; for example, the number of cars parked in the area of the club house and "Pro-Golf Shop," or in the area of the second parking lot used by the members of the smaller course. The number of cars and golf carts is a fair indicator of participation, in that few residents walk to the golf course or to any of Fun City's many other leisure time activities.

Golfing is not only a popular (and prestigious) sport in Fun City, it is an expensive one. Many residents came to Fun City because it promised access to good and inexpensive golf. Many others who were not formally associated with the sport developed a liking for it. Both groups soon discovered that the course at Fun City is mediocre and the expense more than minimal. Indeed, some residents drive to a nearby retirement community where the golf is not only better but less expensive. One golfing family summed it up this way:

> *Mrs. W.:* But it isn't a good golf course, but we're just trapped, you see.
> *Mr. W.:* You have to have a golf cart and you have to pay seventy-five dollars a year for the privilege of using the golf course. And then you have to pay so much per game, see, and if you take it by the year with a golf cart it costs you around four hundred dollars. . . . And you can't play golf during the day, cause the climate don't permit it. Either cold weather or fog or else it's windy and . . . or it's too hot. This is not the ideal climate right here for senior citizens.
> *Dr. J.:* So you don't break ahead unless you play an awful lot of golf?

[2] Most of the course is visible from the street. The above estimate is further supported by a recent article in the *Fun City News* that noted a record turnover of 80 golfers in one day.

The Fun City fairways.

Mr. W.: You have to play almost every day to make anything out of it, you see.

Mrs. W.: We used to when we first came out, play golf more often. Of course, eight years ago you're quite a bit younger you know . . . and then it wasn't quite so expensive, it was only around three hundred dollars, wasn't it dear, for the two of us?

Mr. W.: Fun City said you could play for twenty-five cents a day originally.

Mrs. W.: That's about what it amounted to if you played every day. And it's only those who play every day [that get] their money out of it.

Mr. W.: And that's how he [Fun City's developer] sold a lot of the houses, because of the cheap golf and those that like to play golf you see. But now it has gotten quite expensive.

Mrs. W.: But now when I go out to play nine holes it costs me two-sixty for nine holes and I can go down to Mission which is a gorgeous golf course. . . . I can play golf [there] for two-fifty, ten cents less, whereas here I'm supposed to be getting a deal because I live here and I pay two-sixty.

Square Dance Club

Of the five clubs I have noted the one probably involving the greatest amount of physical exertion is the Square Dance Club.[3] It is also the liveliest and loosest club of all—that is, the least formal and most fun. Contributing to this easiness

---

[3] Golfers invariably use golf carts to cover the course.

is the fact that square dancing is not a daytime but an evening activity, which is held every Wednesday night from 7:30 to 10:30 P.M., in the North Town Hall. The club has an official membership of 250, and dances are relatively well attended, usually by 50 to 60 residents.

Bicycle Club

Finally, there is the Bicycle Club, with 139 members. A description of the club's activities is given in the *Guide*:

> Meetings at 9 A.M. on Tuesday mornings in the parking lot of the Recreation Center. Purpose is recreation. A coffee hour in the Town Hall follows each ride. Special Events: Quarterly dinner parties.

This group is also much less formal and more easygoing than the Camera Club. They seem to enjoy themselves more and are less "uptight." One elderly woman, who has lived nearly seven years in Fun City, stopped to chat and give me a piece of birthday cake (it was her husband's birthday and they were both just returning from their weekly cycling trip). She has logged a total of 8700 miles on these trips. She and her husband used to average about 125 miles a month, but have slowed down considerably of late due to age and failing health. The Bicycle Club generally has a certain easiness about it approximated only by the Square Dance Club. This may be accounted for, at least in part, by an overlapping membership. Bicycle riding and square dancing are two activities that afford the greatest amount of exercise and generally attract the younger or healthier residents. A typical outing draws between 30 and 40 cyclists and usually an equal number of men and women.

Golf, Lawn Bowls, and Shuffleboard

There are several key differences between the major sport club members and the others. To begin with, they are more active. This is especially true (in a competitive sense) of golf, lawn bowls and shuffleboard. Participating residents take their sports seriously. (I was told by gardeners and maintenance crews that lawn bowl games were continued in spite of cold weather and rain.) In short, these three clubs seem to have a higher esprit de corps than many of the others. There were tournaments to play and trophies to win, which in turn led to still another activity: the opportunity to travel to play other "senior citizen" groups. This feature provides for a strong interaction network not only between members, but also between the teams and the outside community. The *Fun City News* (a weekly newspaper), offering an accurate chronicle of sports and other events in Fun City, devotes a regular column to golf, lawn bowls, and shuffleboard. This is not surprising considering the membership of the clubs: lawn bowls, 142 members, and shuffleboard, 130. Add to this the 644 members of the Golf Club and it is clear that a relatively high number of "active" Fun City residents are involved in these three sports.

The members' loyalty to these clubs is rivaled only by that of the card players, who also warrant a regular column in the local paper. The following excerpts from the *Fun City News* give some idea of the important role these activities play in the social life of Fun City's more active residents.

Bowling on the green.

Golf

Only 16 gals turned out for the golf of the Niner's Tuesday: it was a cold, raw windy day and the course was really soaked with water.

The tournament was Low Gross, and winners were:

Flight I, [names of winners]
Flight II, [names of winners]
Flight III, [names of winners]

Following the golf the regular monthly meeting was held, with Audrey J. presiding. Various rules were discussed by Millie O., Rules Chairwoman.

The tournament at Rancho was further outlined and most of the girls are looking forward to participating. A luncheon will follow the golf at Rancho.

Lawn Bowls

Friday, April 23, was the occasion of another first for [Fun City].

It was the visitation of the president of the South-West Division of the American Lawn Bowls Association, Mr. Joseph V. and his lovely wife, Norine. They are members of [the out-of-town] Lawn Bowls Club.

In order to round out the festivities for our visiting dignitary, a game was arranged matching President Joe V., our President Russ O., Vice President, and Lou E., lead against John D., Dave Z., Vice President, and Walter M., lead.

Need I tell you who won? Who's going to be foolish enough to beat a team boasting two presidents? No kidding! We had a wonderful game and the outcome was:

Presidents: 15, Peasants: 12

On Wednesday, April 21, the [out of town] Lawn Bowls Club visited [Fun City] for a day of bowling. The [out of town] Club, along with players from another [out of town] club and with a sprinkling of [Fun City] bowlers playing under their banner, was able to win the honors for the day.

By the way, have you seen the beautiful display of ceramics in the womens' card room? Two of our multi-talented lady bowlers have samples of their handiwork in the exhibit.

On April 26, a sizable group of [Fun City] Bowlers and their wives made the long trek across the hot sands to that oasis in the desert [another retirement community]. Tell you about that in next week's column.

Shuffleboard Club

[Fun City's] shuffleboarders had the first of their summer "fun" games last week. We were guests of [out of town club] the evening of the 21st and true to the [Fun City] tradition our players won the match by a 13 to 11 score.
Making the trip were . . . [names of persons making trip].
Learned of a new shot during the contest. One of our players needed a score on the hammer shot and tried a "double combination with a reverse drift."
This would come under the class of tricky shots that Glen S. should have explained to me. Could be the Club President could have this shot demonstrated at the next club gathering.
Jim D. is putting in many hours making a new "welcome" sign for our visiting clubs. We've seen it and can assure one and all that it is something to be proud of. . . .
We've missed two of our favorite players lately, Art and Berenice Z. They spend so much time globe-trotting, Hawaii to sun bathe, Michigan to fish and many side trips that we didn't realize they were not out of town but instead have been down with the flu. These nice people are all around sportslovers: They golf, lawn bowl, shuffleboard, fish and travel. Send them a card, they'll love hearing from you.

GENERAL CHARACTERISTICS OF THE CLUBS

Another key difference between the major sport clubs and other clubs is that while the members of most other clubs are nonactive, more of the members of the major sport clubs regularly participate in club activities. An indication of this wider membership involvement with respect to golf is that a percentage of the 50 to 75 persons on the fairway on any one day changes from day to day. The same is true for lawn bowling and shuffleboard. I cannot say for certain what percentage of the total membership partakes of these sports, but I can say with some confidence that it is higher than those participating in arts and crafts.

Another important point is that many of the active club members belong to and are active in more than one club at a time. Many of the passive club members also hold membership in more than one club but frequently fail to participate in any. The result of this is that we cannot simply sum the memberships to get the total number of Fun City residents with an official, or participating, membership in clubs. How many belong to one or more clubs remains unknown since the membership lists are unavailable. However, the cleaning lady, maintenance chief, and two of the Fun City's long-term residents independently estimate that there are approximately five hundred active club members. This figure supports my estimate based upon numerous observations. While the distribution of club members is in question, the total active membership can be fixed with some confidence.

> *Mr. X.*: Out of six thousand, I'd say five hundred participate in this and that. The rest stay home.
> *Mr. D.*: The rest stay home and they're busy in their homes . . . and they relax.
> *Mr. X.*: You saw the weekly program, didn't you?
> *Dr. J.*: Yeah, there seemed like a lot of things to do.
> *Mr. D.*: No, no. [They're not participating.] You take away the five hundred that's doing it—from shuffleboard, from bowling, from ceramics, from painting, from concerts, from meetings, take the five hundred away and it'll be dead.

What are some of the other characteristics of Fun City clubs? First, some of the clubs provide activities that stimulate the active involvement of nonactive members. I have in mind here the Ceramics, Sewing, and Camera Clubs. In the first two, the women frequently take projects home to work on and come to the activity center itself only infrequently. Some of the Camera Club members, while they do not attend formal meetings (or attend them only infrequently), take lots of pictures. In the same way, Card Club members frequently have home games with friends who may or may not be fellow club members.

Second, the club get-togethers, in addition to being an occasion for the activity itself (or for a formal meeting) are usually accompanied by a coffee-and-cake social hour. This too, provides a setting for the initiation of more meaningful forms of interaction.

Shuffleboard players.

Third, participation in many of these clubs, such as golf, lawn bowls, and shuffleboard, occasions visits to social clubs in other places. This results in team members meeting the greater public, competing for prizes, increasing interactions between team-mates and others, and building self-esteem.

Finally, some clubs, while providing essentially for leisure time activities, are service clubs as well. For example, the wood shop members made glass-fronted wooden holders for small oxygen tanks that were placed around the area in case of emergency. Members of the Drama Club contributed the oxygen tanks and also put on benefits for a rest home that was located on the outskirts of Fun City and adjacent to the Mortuary. The Ceramics Club contributed framed works to decorate the ladies' clubroom. All of these good works on the part of active residents help to contribute to building the participants' self-esteem and the clubs' esprit de corps.

SERVICE, FRATERNAL, AND POLITICAL CLUBS

Apart from clubs dealing with leisure, sports, and public service, there are numerous fraternal, political, and religious organizations in Fun City, with varying memberships. The following are some examples of such clubs with large (paper) memberships: American Legion Post, 250 members; Masonic Club, 490 members; Eastern Star (Miriam Chapter), 302 members; Republican Assembly, 549 members; Democratic Club, 175 members; Property Owners United, 700 members; Veterans of World War I Barracks, 276 members; Shrine Club, 200 members. Some smaller memberships in this category are the Sons of the American Revolution, 50 members; Daughters of the American Revolution, 50 members; and the Rotary Club, 62 members.

CHURCH GROUPS

Church membership in Fun City is listed in the guide as follows: Catholic Church, 700 members; Lutheran Church, 200 members; Methodist Church, 450 members; Progressive Reform Judaism, 70 members; Temple Beth Sholom, 125 members; United Church of [Fun City], 550 members; Seventh Day Adventist Church, 20 members; and the Church of Jesus Christ of Latter Day Saints, 60 members.

Church membership and/or participation can be a mixed blessing. On the one hand, quite apart from its religious functions, the Church provides a social setting and many volunteer activities for its members. Many Church members who attend religious services infrequently, consistently attend social functions and volunteer projects. This is especially true among the small Jewish congregation, a number of whom volunteered that they were agnostics or avowed atheists.

While there are social benefits to be derived from Church membership there are, for many, also untoward consequences. For example, there are in Fun City many Masons, nearly all of whom belong to the same church. Apart from the usual expectations of congregations for a show of unity, all Masons are "brothers" with obligations above and beyond those usually associated with church going. For example, they are expected to attend the funerals of their brothers, and many do. This results in large segments of this particular congregation attending a funeral or two almost every week. Social isolates, casual churchgoers, or social function goers of other congregations do not have to contend with the problem of death in quite the same way. This provides a kind of insulation which can only be viewed as "functional." Nor is this only my evaluation. Masons, at least those I spoke to, while they were glad to do their duty were not gladdened by the prospect of attending one funeral after another. The dedication of Masons to Fun City religious life was extraordinary. According to one army chaplain who is currently active in Fun City religious life, the residents' participation in religious functions left something to be desired.

If there are not as many churchgoers in Fun City as one would anticipate (and I have this appraisal from several sectors, in addition to the chaplain) there is no paucity of churches. Indeed, there were about a dozen for approximately six thousand people within an area of about one square mile. However, not all religious denominations have their own buildings, and a few of the smaller ones use the facilities in the Town Hall.

LARGE PASSIVE MEMBERSHIP CLUBS

There are several Fun City clubs characterized by large membership and low participation, such as the Women's Club with 596 members, the Travel Club with 850 members, the Slim and Trim Club with 395 members, and the Swim Club with 106 members.

THE ROLE OF EMPLOYMENT

A cursory look at Fun City seems to reveal little in the way of employment opportunities. There are few retail establishments, no industry, civil service, or other institutionalized forms of employment. A closer look reveals that while not plentiful, jobs are more numerous than one would first suppose. While there are some jobs for residents, the "goodness of fit" between the applicant's expertise and the task's requirements is frequently bizarre. Retired admirals paint houses, retired colonels pump gas or transcribe math problems into braille for the blind, while housewives act as realtors. Other well-to-do residents work as handymen or gardeners, or in a neighboring town at a discount department store. While it is true that most Fun City residents live on fixed incomes and work to supplement these, many others who work for poor pay at unskilled jobs are independently wealthy.[5] Furthermore, it seems that at least some of these marginally employed residents are not socially active in Fun City's clubs or organizations—in other

---

[5] One newspaper survey I was told of revealed the average fixed income to be $8,000 per year.

words, are not only marginally employed but are "marginal men" by Fun City standards.

Some residents are not retired at all. Several work full time in the local post office; a postman's neighbor commutes 90 miles (one way) daily to a neighboring metropolitan area to a full-time job (he was planning to retire soon), and several others are employed full or part time as realtors. The staff of the *Fun City News* are all Fun City residents, and a few others are employed part time as college professors. Exactly how many persons are employed full or part time remains unknown. The number of those employed full time is surely very small, while the number of those who are employed part time, work as odd jobs, or donate their time to charities is substantial.

An example of such charitable work is the Fun City Players, a volunteer drama group. One of its activities is to stage occasional plays for the benefit of residents. In addition, they sometimes volunteer to put on productions for the entertainment of the patients at the adjacent nursing home, which is situated between the Fun City Ambulance Service and the Mortuary. Upon attending a late afternoon performance in the dining room (dinner was being served during the performance), I witnessed the following scene. Many patients were eating their meal, frequently with the assistance of the nursing home aids, and paying no attention whatever to the play. Others nodded half asleep with their backs to the performers, while the rest stared blankly out the window. In fact, of the twenty or so persons comprising the audience, only three seemed to be paying any attention whatever to the performance. This was especially telling when we consider that it was a one-act, four-party situation comedy that lasted about twenty minutes from opening to finale.

What did the players make of this audience response? They were gratified. They told each other how well it had all gone and how well it had been received. They were pleased that they were able to help those less fortunate by entertaining them and felt they really should stage performances there more often in light of so appreciative a response. One might well ask how a misperception of this order is possible. I believe any answer to this question must include a recognition of the fact that the more active residents want to feel not only active but needed. In order to fulfill this need, they have to involve themselves in some sort of volunteer or paid activity. While paid activities are (for the residents) by definition gainful, or meaningful activities, volunteer work is somewhat more ambiguously defined. In order to dispel this ambiguity and build self-esteem, volunteer work is almost always undertaken on behalf of a third party and as a group effort. This provides not only an interactional network for dispelling boredom but also the reciprocal reinforcement members need to view volunteer work as a needed and consequently meaningful group activity.

The stage performance I have described was an attempt on the part of Fun City's more active residents to neutralize for themselves and others the negative connotations that they attached to the phrase "Senior Citizen." Residents felt that they were not what society at large took them to be—persons who should now "disengage" from the social arena because of their inability to contribute meaningfully to their own needs or the needs of others. Active members considered themselves not only capable of meeting their own needs, but able to help others as well.

In short, the ardent pursuit of these volunteer or unskilled forms of employment by wealthy and formally elitist segments of society may be accounted for, at least in part, as follows: Work, among those holding a work ethic, is the source of one's identity and self-esteem. This is especially true of those ascribing to "the Protestant ethic and the spirit of capitalism" and a rugged individualism and a strong anti-welfare–state ideology. "Work makes life sweet" is no idle expression to residents whose biographies read like Horatio Alger stories. Such persons find the abrupt transition from a work to a leisure ethic especially difficult. The search for work is a search not only for an end to excess time for persons who were formerly busy and gainfully employed, but also for the continuous source of self-esteem and the key to maintaining one's prior identity. The identity crisis accompanying the transition from one stage of the life cycle to another is always difficult. At these junctures one needs to be "cooled out" of one set of values into another. This cooling-out process is particularly trying in old age, notwithstanding the planners' efforts to build into the retirement community mechanisms designed to facilitate this transition.

CONCLUSION

In summary, it may be said of Fun City's more active residents that on first entering upon an "active way of life" they join many clubs and organizations. In time they "drop out," from either lack of interest or failing health, and while maintaining a paper membership in many clubs, actively participate in only one or two. In many instances club members are nonparticipants. Finally, activities are rarely concerned with intellectual pursuits and contribute primarily to a "passive way of life."

There are, however, occasional exceptions to this pattern. Some small segment of active residents, mostly women, initiate and maintain an active membership in many clubs over time. The following is the verbatim account of one such woman (a Fun City pioneer) who, among other pursuits, holds a high-echelon position in the local D.A.R. Chapter, the Ladies' Club, and the California Republican Assembly, and is also an active member of two school boards in neighboring towns.

Mrs. R.: Well, we moved here in 1963. April 1st of '63—we were among the first residents. And we came from what is a lovely, was a lovely place . . . and my husband . . . We went to [another retirement community] first and loved the idea but it was too hot. We couldn't stand it. And we said, well, we will wait and see what the place in California looks like. And so we came out here and bought the lot. Oh, there was nothing. . . . We came here when the office was a little bit of a room, you might say, and the bulldozers were working on the ground. This was all farmland, you know. And we bought our lot—there wasn't a house, there wasn't anything. . . .

And one of the first things, naturally, that we had to do was organize a church. So, the first church here was the United Church of [Fun City]. That is the old Congregational church. I am a Presbyterian and have always been, but there was going to be no Presbyterian Church here so we affiliated with the United Church of [Fun City] . . . Then, I'll tell you the first years were pretty discouraging. I bawled every day for six weeks. I looked out my front yard and all I could see, my husband had, eight hundred feet I think he said, to put in the water system—you know the sprinkling system in the yard. The dust was blowing a hurricane. The house was full of dirt. It was very depressing. And I thought, where has he brought me? And we had a lovely place in Southern California with one-half acre of ground, and it was just lovely. And honest to goodness, all you could see out here was a bunch of white roofs. There wasn't a tree. There wasn't a bush. We had to start planting as soon as we got the water system in and then he put in the lawn. And then he. . . . I want to tell you something. You wouldn't believe this place today to what it was only eight years ago. There was nothing. . . .

You see this town looks good because these houses are approximately the same age, don't you see. We don't have any slum area or any bad, broken-down looking houses. And another thing, everybody keeps their yards up, because if they didn't the neighbors would give them what for. So really it is a well-cared-for town.

Well, then one of the next things we had to have was a Woman's Club. You can't live in a town without a woman's club. So in 'sixty-three we organized the Woman's Club. And we said, well, we will call for a meeting and if we don't get fifty people there why we will know that Fun City is not ready for a woman's club. Well, we had three hundred and some. The biggest woman's club that was ever organized at the start. And this last year we had six hundred and seven members. And it is one of the liveliest organizations in town. We have beautiful programs. We have a wonderful tea at the beginning of each meeting. That girl [Mrs. K.] was my stage (designed the stage decor). I was the president this past year and she did the stage decorations. And they were fabulous. That girl is something. And she made my press book and it is something. It is just simply a work of art.

And we do a lot of philanthropic work. We give scholarships to [Jonesville] . . . you know, little old [Jonesville] over here. It is a very poor town. And last year we gave eighteen hundred dollars in scholarships. This year we gave one thousand dollars. Our students have gone on, really they have done exceptionally well. Now one of our students three years ago was a boy named Jackson. Now his grades were not good, but he had talent. And we gave him a scholarship for extra talent but not scholarship. And last night I saw a whole bunch of his pictures. They are simply fabulous. That boy has just done wonders. And then that little Paul Jones, you know, that we gave a scholarship to, he took dress designing, and I attended a wedding over in Jonesville in the Baptist Church—he decorated the church, he made the girl's wedding dress, he made all the bridesmaid's dresses, and it was the most gratifying thing you have ever seen. He is a little colored boy and he never could have gone on if we hadn't of helped him. We gave him a five hundred dollar scholarship. And now, well, he is just doing great. And this Samuel Jackson, he is about seven feet something tall, and as I say a poor student but loaded with capabilities. And now he has received a scholarship from an advertising agency so that he is going to get a good job and he can further his studies. You see, he is going to take up commercial art. Oh, honestly, his pictures are unbelievable. . . . Now this year we are giving two nursing scholarships. And it's because we really aren't as stupid as we are stupid-looking. We gave nursing scholarships because we expect these kids to come back in about twenty years and take care of us.

Dr. J.: Well, I can see there are a lot of clubs and activities.

Mrs. R.: Eighty, we only have eighty clubs. So that there is plenty to do for everybody who wants something to do. They can find their niche. They can do something. They can either have a hobby or—but let me tell you something.

When you talk to some of them and they say "Oh, this is the worst town we ever saw, they aren't friendly, you can't meet anybody." . . . that's not true. You get out of a place what you put into it. And you can't expect to sit in your front room and people are going to come and wait on you and drag you out to these different things. You have to put forth some effort. And that's true in any community. I don't care whether it is a retirement community or a bustling all-age community—the same thing is true [anywhere].

3 / The invisible majority:
A passive way of life

THE LEISURE TIME PURSUITS OF NONACTIVE RESIDENTS

The previous discussion has outlined some of the more salient features of the social interaction patterns of Fun City's more active residents. What is retirement like for the inactive or non-club–member? It has already been pointed out that for active members (depending on the activity) participation did not necessarily lead to "an active way of life." With respect to Fun City's nonactive citizens the pursuit of leisure time activities is best summarized as the social organization of a passive way of life. One resident summed up a typical day as follows:

Mr. N.: Well, for me a typical day is—I get up at six A.M. in the morning generally, get the newspaper. I look at the financial statement and see what my stocks have done. I generally fix my own breakfast because my wife has, can eat different than I do. So I have my own breakfast—maybe some cornflakes with soy milk in it—milk made out of soybeans that they sell in the health food store. And uh, then at eight A.M. my wife gets up. The dog sleeps with her all night. And uh, she feeds the dog. Then the dog wants me to go out and sit on the patio—get the sun and watch the birds and stuff in our backyard and we have quite a few rabbits back in there. And I finish my paper there. And then she sits and she looks at me. She'll bark a little bit. And uh, then she'll go to my wife, stand by my wife and bark at her. She wants me to go back to bed. So I have to go back to bed with her. So about eight-thirty A.M. I go back to bed again with my dog for about an hour. And then I get up and I read. And then I walk up around here and I go over to oh, the Mayfair [supermarket] and sit there and talk to people. We go over to the bank. They have a stock-room over there. For people that own stock. We discuss stocks and events of the day. And then I come home and maybe have lunch if I want to or not— it doesn't make any difference. *In fact, down here it doesn't make any difference when you eat or when you sleep. Because you're not going any place. You're not doing anything. And uh, if I'm up all night reading and sleep all day, what's the difference.* [Emphasis added.] But then, I'll sit around and read and maybe a neighbor will come over or I'll go over to a neighbor's and sit down and talk about something. And lots of times, we go over to a neighbor's and we play cards 'til about five P.M. and then we come home and have our dinner. And the evening is . . . we are generally glued to the television until bedtime comes. And that's our day.

Dr. J.: Is that more or less what your friends and neighbors do?

Mr. N.: Some of them do. Some of them don't do that much.

31

The retirement activities of another resident is encapsulated in the following dialogue. The opening line refers to the reasons for poor attendance at language classes and why they were frequently cancelled.

Mr. P.: So you see here, the problem with people, elderly people, you know, you must remember their physical condition. Their eyes are not too good. Their memory's not too good. They don't hear so good. So you know what they do? A lot of them art [attend arts and crafts] and a lot of them play cards. . . .

Mr. X.: Out of six thousand I'd say five hundred participate [in clubs and activities] and the rest stay home.

Mr. P.: The rest stay home and they're busy in their homes and they relax. . . .

Dr. J.: What do they do at home?

Mr. P.: Well, the most of them lay down in the afternoon, you know, for a couple of hours.

Mr. X.: They're aching; they're aching.

Mr. P.: And the . . . now my life is organized differently. We came here almost five years ago. In the morning, I get up, have breakfast, and it takes me a couple of hours before I'm through with my paper. Then I'm out around here. Take a walk. In the evening I play records and do a lot of reading you see.

Mr. X.: He goes to the library every day and picks up lots of stuff. He's a very cultured man.

Mr. P.: My wife she can't read because of her eyesight—bad. Now in the evening I have one class a week now. They have another class here on Tuesday. It's a literature class. It's poorly attended too, I guess.

Mr. X.: Do they still have the language classes?

Mr. S.: No . . . yes, they have German . . . and Spanish . . . three times a week.

Mr. X: I thought they had . . .

Mr. P.: Spanish, German, no French. Spanish and German. I don't attend, although I should take Spanish, but I don't. Because it's in the afternoon, and I lay down again. So you see, my life is organized . . . which it satisfies me, you see, and then sometimes we get together and play a game of cards . . . no gambling ways, you know, a social game. And that's the way we spend . . . [our time]. And that's the retirement.

HEALTH, TEMPERAMENT, AND INACTIVITY

Inactive and nonclub members fall into two basic groups, those who want to be socially active but for one reason or another feel that they cannot participate, and those residents who have long since adopted nonmembership in formal organizations as a life style. With the first set, the most frequent reason given for their inability to participate in an active way of life is poor health. Strokes, heart conditions, poor eyesight, loss of hearing, and a variety of other serious and lesser ailments restrict the activity of many Fun City residents and their prospects for establishing ongoing forms of meaningful interactions. The wife of one resident who belongs to a card club and used to read a lot is now unable to participate in these activities because of poor eyesight. Now she spends most of her time at home sleeping. Another resident tells of how he cannot join in club activities because all of the facilities are air conditioned and the air conditioning aggravates his arthritis. In fact, during the winter months from about 3:00 P.M. on, he customarily takes to his home and stays there until about 10:00 A.M. the next morning. Most of the time is spent watching television. Other residents are easily tired, and taking the dog for a walk is an activity that is followed by a long rest period. Poor health accounts for a large segment of nonjoiners and once-active "drop-outs."

The subject of poor health and health facilities is a frequent topic of conversation among Fun City residents. Apart from discussing recent deaths, strokes, or other serious ailments or health problems of residents, the most popular complaint is the poor ambulance service available to stricken residents, and the absence of emergency or major medical facilities within the boundaries of Fun City. While some residents gave positive testimonials to the fast and courteous service rendered by Fun City's volunteer ambulance service (available to the residents at a yearly fee) others have little faith in this service and hope they never have to test the credibility of the stories. While Fun City has four doctors, two dentists, two optometrists, and a chiropractor, most of whom are housed within the Fun City Medical Clinic, there are no emergency or in-patient hospital facilities for Fun City residents. Hospitalization for a serious illness is possible only at nearby and not-so-nearby cities. A hospital facility for Fun City, though long in the planning stages, has never left the drawing boards.

In addition to failing health, "occupational hazards" also play a role in one's reluctance to become or remain an active participant. Retired doctors, lawyers, or accountants are besieged by club members and friends for free medical, legal, or tax advice. Professionals who have not practiced for some time consider themselves neither qualified nor inclined to give free advice. With the lowered tolerance for annoyance that comes with age and poor health, the one-time active members feel that they are constantly being used by the other residents. The ultimate solution to this problem is their gradual withdrawal from club activities. Such persons frequently maintain a paper membership and inactive status.

Other nonparticipating residents who are not "drop-out" have chosen, as part of their former life style, not to join clubs or participate in planned activities. One resident put it this way:

> *Mr. O.*: Then I lived on F. Avenue. I had a business there for many years on W. Boulevard and K.—K. Avenue and W. I had a store right there in the heart of town. I used to know everybody there. After that I didn't go there. And they say the problem is this way . . . the trouble is with a lot of Jewish people [the informant was Jewish] . . . if you don't belong to their organization or you don't believe like they do, you're an outcast, more or less. I never joined their temple. I'm not religious, and I don't play the part, you see. To me it's the principle like, so a lot of them did not associate with it. They had their own parties, their own this . . . and I'm not an assimilationist either, I'm not an assimilationist but I do . . . I'm not religious, that's all. The same thing here. They try to get you in, and they try with all kinds of talk, you know, but to me it doesn't appeal, the whole idea.

TELEVISION AS A LEISURE TIME PURSUIT

What other forms of leisure did Fun City's inactive residents engage in to "kill time"? We have already mentioned the importance of card playing, either as a formal planned activity in the Activity Center, or as an informal pastime in one's home. However, the importance of television has not yet received the emphasis it deserves. Fun City residents watch television frequently, in the morning, afternoon, and evening. In fact, for many of the nonactive residents (by far the majority of all Fun City residents) it is the major leisure time pursuit. Television also helps to keep them in touch with the outside world. Card playing and telvision watching are two activities that vie for most residents' major allotment of time. One resident summarizes the importance of television this way:

> *Dr. J.:* How about those people who aren't in the, uh, very active or even members of the clubs?
>
> *Mr. N.:* Well, television has made a lot of things possible that wasn't true with my father and my grandfather. Oftentimes I wonder about my grandfather who lived in a farm in Pennsylvania—what in the world he did with himself. Get up and work all day and evening came and he would eat, and uh, what did he do? He would go to bed on an old straw mattress. And of course, they got up quite early. But gee, a life like that I just couldn't take. I think it would drive me nuts. I think television has been a great thing with shut-ins and people like that. Because they still have pretty good programs . . . I watch it lots in the afternoon—different programs. And we have cable in here, you know, where we get fine reception here. And uh, *oh its one of these places that it would be hard to maintain, I think, without television. People would feel too isolated, too away from things. Regardless of the age you become you kind of want to get in the millstream a little bit, you know.* [Emphasis added.] So with television and radio, at night when I've slept too much in the daytime I have a radio by my bed. I have an ear thing. And I put that between my pillows. And I listen to that all night long. The news, you know. So, what's the difference. I might just as well listen to that. I don't care if I sleep or not. It doesn't make any difference. Sometimes I get up. I have one of those recliner chairs. And I sit in that and read and fall asleep and maybe sleep there for a couple of hours. What difference does it make? I've accomplished nothing down here . . . There's a few people in the evening [out for a walk]. Like my wife— my wife walks the dog in the evening. I walk her in the daytime. And there's a few couples out that you meet, you know, that like to walk in the cool of the evening. But most of them are glued to their television.

THE RANGE OF ACTIVITY AND INACTIVITY

It is generally true that the extent of a resident's social life in Fun City is directly related to his or her social life prior to retiring. Persons with an active social life before coming to Fun City continue to be active, while those with inactive life styles prior to retirement tend to continue in that mode. One active resident summed up this position as follows:

> *Mrs. O.:* Yes, well, it's like any other community. You don't change coming here. You are what you were before you came. If you were a gregarious outgoing person and liked things, you'd like it here. If you weren't, you'd hate it. . . . It's what people bring with them.
>
> I would say that there have been two times in my life when I felt that need for inner strength. One was in the years when I was a Girl Scout director. I was a camp director for many years. And to be on your own out in the wilderness with a group of little kids you gotta have a lot of inner strength to be

able to take it. *In other words, the loneliness.* [Emphasis added.] Well, what prepared me for this was the fact that I grew up out in the wilds in North Dakota in the prairie country where we didn't have lots of people around us all the time. You had to have times when you had to form your own amusement.

And there are many city-bred people who don't have that. They've always been used to canned amusement and entertainment. So they don't have recourse to books and music and whatever it is you need. Well, that's what happened here. And it's more so I think as people get older or if they become immobile or if they are ill, which a lot of 'em do here, and they begin to feel sorry for themselves.

I have neighbors on both sides of me that just drive me mad. I don't think this woman has ever had visitors or visited. I'm the only person I know that ever goes in there. They never been down at the Town Hall. She's going almost totally blind now. She'd been diabetic but she's been that all her life. And now you see this one over here is a fairly young woman, a beautiful woman in her early fifties but she's almost a mental case because she babies herself so and imagines that she's sick. Oh, she married late in life. And oh, it's just a . . . I get so irritated with these people. I've got 'em all around me. The one across the street is just as bad. But they expect me to come to them all the time and of course like a nut I do. And I run around and go to see them all.

Dr. J.: How long have they been here?

Mrs. O.: Oh, they've all been here ten years [since Fun City's opening]. So this is an old neighborhood. And the one across the street kitty-cornered, and they are very wealthy people. They were married late in life, an old maid and an old bachelor who were schoolmates. And when his old mother died he finally came out here. He made a fortune. . . .

Now these, there's four of 'em right around here who have all been so concerned with themselves and their health that they made life miserable for their mates. But I tell you I believe they'd always been that way. I don't believe you change just because you get a little bit older. And I'm just living here but I've always liked it wherever I'd been. And I've been to some of the most God-forsaken places you ever heard of.

As Mrs. O. astutely notes, not everyone is a Thoreau, nor did most of Fun City's residents formerly reside at Walden Pond. In short, they are ill-equipped to deal with Fun City's general state of geographical and social isolation. Many residents are in fact lonely. However, Mrs. O. is perhaps overly harsh in her appraisal of her neighbors' inability to cope successfully with their environment. Mrs. O. is relatively young and in good health. Most of her neighbors are neither. Apart from this, living in Fun City requires that one call forth all of one's "inner resources," and these are not qualities that one cultivates in the metropolitan environment from which most of Fun City's residents were recruited. In fact, the general mode of adaptation characteristic of the urban-acclimatized person is what Simmel referred to as the "blasé attitude."

It is ironic that the cultivation of the "blasé attitude" which one adopts in self-defense in the metropolis, because one is otherwise unable to cope with the extent and intensity of stimuli, should be the same adaptive technique used by Fun City residents. This I feel can be at least partially explained by noting the reason for the urban dweller's withdrawal. It is the self's inability to integrate the profusion and diversity of stimuli that causes the withdrawal—it is because of the threat to the self that one withdraws. The threat to the self is also present in Fun City, but comes from another quarter. Here one tends to withdraw from all but the most casual and innocuous forms of interaction in order not to give or take offense, which leads Fun City to appear to be a nice, friendly, safe place to live. It is this image that one buys into and does one's best to maintain. This aspect will be discussed in greater detail in Chapter 4.

Although it was generally true that the extent of one's social life in Fun City closely resembles the extent of one's social activity prior to retiring, this general formulation requires some qualification. Persons who were formerly active would not go on being active at any price. Temperament was another important factor. For example, one might expect active persons to seek membership in various social clubs. This was not always true. Formerly active persons, characterized by "low key"[1] temperaments, would forgo the ready-made social gatherings provided by social clubs (in which they were otherwise interested) because their memberships were characterized by what "low key" residents referred to as "high key" and/or "uptight persons." "Low key" active persons prefer to remain relatively inactive for a period of time, and wait for interactions to emerge with other formerly active or inactive "low key" residents. "High key" active residents, on the other hand, tend to seek out other "high key" types, who are recruited almost exclusively from the ranks of formerly active persons.

The range of involvement among Fun City's active and passive residents is illustrated in the following account:

Mr. K.: But we do have them [inactive or non-club–members] and like, well on both sides of us here [as neighbors]. Now, all she does [one neighbor] is play bridge. Now, all he does is go to the Royal Inn and have a few beers. That is the extent of their activities.

Mrs. R.: Well, of course, tell him about the bridge. Oh, this town . . .

Mr. K.: Oh, the bridge club is absolutely out of its mind about bridge.

Mrs. R.: They just play bridge.

Mr. K.: Oh, this lady here, and the next one too, they just dash out and play bridge.

Mrs. K.: You see, when we first came here we had bridge clubs, friends, you know. And then we had the neighborhood bridge. Well to me, it was taking so much of my time, and I couldn't concentrate on it—I'd rather do things that I couldn't do while I was teaching. And so I got into bicycling, and golfing, and all these things more of the active type. [Mrs. K. is younger than the average resident.]

Mrs. R.: I don't play a bit of bridge. In fact, I don't know how. And I cannot afford to waste my time all day. Some of these people start at nine A.M. in the morning. They play until night. I cannot waste my time. I have to be doing something that I think is constructive for my community and myself.

Mrs. K.: I am so glad to hear that because they thought I was terrible. I was

---

[1] *High key* persons are characterized more by aggressive and pretentious personalities and seek to achieve goals through influence peddling or intimidation strategies. As a group they are best characterized as operating with "the hard sell."

Low key persons are characterized more by nonaggressive or oppressive behavior, are much less pretentious, and seek to achieve goals more through well-modulated, reasoned argument and what can be best summarized as "the soft sell."

dropping out of the bridge here and the bridge there, you know. And I just said to myself, "When I get old and can't do all these other things, well, then maybe I'll sit down and play bridge with you."

Mrs. R.: Oh, when I get old and can't do anything I'm boing to read—catch up on my reading that I am about 20 years behind on.

Mrs. K.: Same here.

Mr. K.: And add to that a gentleman next door is a retired colonel from the Army. He and his wife just have relatives up north that they visit. And they visit over across in Star Beach. And he spends all his time transferring braille—uh, mathematics into braille for the blind.

Mrs. R.: Well, now, that's good.

Mr. K.: That's all he does, but he works hard at it and he's good. But he's one of the few people that is accepted by the Library of Congress to do this translation. But math is tough to do. And he is, he is trained in it, and he spends all of his time doing this.

Mrs. R.: Well, I don't care what else he does. Why, that is the most humanitarian thing. . . .

Mr. K.: And he'll come out and smoke a cigar or pipe around the yard a little bit. And they make a trip up to Monterey about once a year. And they go over to Star Beach. And then they'll . . . she is a Blue Lady [volunteer] up in the Air Force Hospital.

Mrs. R.: Once a week she goes.

Mr. K.: Once a week, on Tuesday, because she began to lose her sight and hearing.

Mrs. R.: Is that why he got into braille?

Mr. K.: Well, I don't know. It's just Sam is a sort of peculiar guy and just all of a sudden he started doing this braille.

Mrs. R.: Well, It think it's marvelous.

Dr. J.: How long has he been here and how long has he been doing the braille?

Mr. K.: He's been here the same . . . he came a month ahead of us. [They have been there for seven years.] . . . And next door to them. Those people there, I don't believe they leave the house. I never see them leave the house. I don't even know them. I don't believe they leave the house.

Mrs. K.: Except to go down to the movies, the movies down here. [A movie is shown in Town Hall once a month by the American Legion.] They go down to that. But they are content to stay home and sit around. . . .

Mr. K.: This lady across the street lost her husband not too long ago and all she does is take care of that forest over there [her shrubbery]. So I'm just trying to give you . . . Now, we have a retired admiral down the street that's a retired medical admiral. The old admiral, all he does is drink booze. So figure it out.

Now, down the street there is another gentleman that is an ardent golfer. He can do anything. He plays the organ, he plays the piano, he's in the square dancers. He's the secretary of the club. Al Brown.

Mrs. R.: Al Brown? Oh yeah.

Mrs. K.: He's secretary in the Civic Association. And anything he does he can make it turn. And what's he doing? He's painting houses around town. He likes to paint. And he may make an extra dollar. And we kid him about having his tin cans out in the yard and so forth.

Mrs. K.: And if they go on a trip we'll say, "Oh, you dug up all your tin cans again."

Mr. K.: They'll go on a trip down to . . . they went to New Orleans and they were gone, what—ten or twelve days. And they lived at the best. You know, they had a big ball. They came home and enjoyed themselves. That's the way they do it.

Dr. J.: Does he still belong to all these things or does he . . .

Mrs. K.: Yes, he does that in-between. And, if he's painting one day and he's square dancing that night, he doesn't feel like square dancing he doesn't go, you see. You don't have to be regimented here.

Dr. J.: Yes, I see. You just kind of play it by ear.

Mrs. K.: That's right, you play it by ear. . . .

Mrs. R.: The way you feel.

Mrs. K.: The way you feel is right.

Mr. K.: Like she pointed out, you go into some of these places and they "can"[2] you right in there. Now, the only time I figure that I want to be put in one of those places is when I am incapable of getting out and doing things.

Mrs. R.: That's right.

Dr. J.: Well, you've been living in Fun City for about seven or eight years, and you've been working until recently. Now here's this other person you're telling me about—he sometimes paints houses for whatever reason. How many people do you think there are who are semi-retired and do a little work here?

Mrs. R.: You mean have little jobs

Dr. J.: Yeah, who make a little money here and there.

Mrs. R.: Two-thirds of them, quite a lot [off the cuff estimate].

Mr. K.: At least half of them [off the cuff estimate]. They'll have [to] do something. Some of them work down at the K-Market and the gas station. They'll get—well, there is one fella who is retired, a lieutenant-commander in the Navy down here that—uh, I know he's got sufficient [is independently wealthy], but he goes down to the gas station and works down at the gas station for a lousy two bucks an hour. We have a colonel, retired, over here, that full colonel that works down at the gas station. As a matter of fact he came to the post office to work for a while. He just couldn't take it, with his legs, it was killing him. He's probably 56 or 57 years old.[3]

Mrs. R.: Well, and then we have, you know, Smith, still runs his law offce. And Al B. and his son are accountants, you know, they still work. And we have several of, oh, quite a number, who do people's tax things.

Mr. & Mrs. K.: Oh, yes.

Mr. K.: We have a lot of tax consultants.

Mrs. R.: You'd be surprised how many people. They might not work all the time, and they might not have a real job, as you call it, but they do something to supplement their income. Because you know a lot of people came here with the idea that this was going to be a cheap place to live. Now this is not a cheap place to live by any means. And so, a lot of them, in order to do the things they want—they could have existed without doing it—but when you want to take a trip someplace with the travel club or you want to go here or you want to buy this, if they figure that if they can earn a little it just helps out. Now look at Floyd T. Do you know Floyd T.?

Mr. K.: I know the name, I don't . . .

Mrs. R.: Why, he paints people's houses. He works . . . but they go for three months. They just got back from a three-months' tour. . . . That's another thing. These people have house trailers. And boy do they travel. They go away for two and three months at a time. And then come back. . . .

---

[2] "Can" means "package" you into an environmental setting according to some prearranged formula or set of social expectations.

[3] A number of military personnel were retired relatively early. A number went from the military into civil service, especially post office jobs, before retiring fully.

TRAVEL: AN OCCASIONAL BREAK WITH THE
PASSIVE WAY OF LIFE

We have considered two major shared activities of club members and non-members: card playing and television watching. A third less time-consuming shared activity is travel. Travel for Fun City residents usually takes one of the following forms: organized travel in groups, planned by agents of the travel club, or informal individually initiated sorties by residents. The latter are usually undertaken in the company of at least a second party.

Travel arrangements for large groups of 30 to 50 persons are usually arranged by travel club agents. Most travel club excursions are one-day outings to the metropolitan center (usually to see some "cultural event") or to local tourist attractions. One elderly gentleman, whose wife frequently goes on these outings (he has difficulty walking and does not travel, nor does he actively participate in any of the clubs or organizations) gave me the following examples of trips and their costs: A trip to the metropolitan center to see Liberace, including the price of admission and round-trip fare, was eleven dollars; to the metropolis and back to see the film, "Song of Norway" was eight dollars, and a trip to a local tourist attraction was, he believed, about eleven or twelve dollars. My informant's wife has been to see "Song of Norway" four times. All of these outings he took to be both interesting ways to spend the day and a bargain. However, while the expense of these trips seems reasonable to some, it seems extravagant to others.

Mr. S.: I'll tell you what they lack here. We've got travel clubs . . .

Mr. X.: Oh, we do a lot of traveling.

Mr. S.: . . . the Travel Club is organized in a different way—different than in other places. Now in [the metropolis], the Senior Citizens' group arranges traveling . . . here . . . there . . . which it costs you very little. Here when you travel it costs you a lot of money. . . .

Mr. X.: Three buses come up here . . . Greyhound buses. They travel here at least three times a week.

Mr. D.: They cost you a lot of money.

Dr. J.: Do a lot of people travel?

Mr. D.: A lot of people.

Mr. X.: Well, in their younger days, they were busy working, business . . . and now they're taking advantage of it. With me, you couldn't buy me a ticket, I've seen it. I'm going to take my walk and then I'm going to the market.

Mr. D.: Yeah, go ahead. I'll see you there maybe.

An interesting aside on travel club arrangements was given by one informant who noted that: "Over there [a neighbor of his], he's vice-president of the Travel Club. Well his wife doesn't like to ride in the car. She'd rather ride in the bus. So he always organizes trips to Las Vegas [a favorite trip of theirs]."

While it is impossible to ascertain the exact number of Fun City residents who go on one-day excursions (including one-day shopping trips to neighboring towns), or the frequency with which they engage in this activity, it is clearly the most popular form of travel. Many (perhaps most) are non-Travel–Club members who simply take a day's drive to the beach or to neighboring resort towns for a "good meal" or "the baths." Another form of one-day (or weekend) outing is visiting relatives, usually children or grandchildren. As I have noted, a substantial portion of Fun City residents come from the adjacent metropolitan area. Others came to Fun City from out-of-state to be closer to their children. However, visits to relatives, or from them, are not as frequent as one might have supposed, and certainly not as frequent as the residents would have liked.

> And our kids really don't want us. They like us. They respect us. And they'd do anything for us. But they have their life to live and it is entirely different from ours. All I have to do is go back when I was a kid. I didn't want my dad going where I did, doing a lot of the things I did. And uh, I never expected it when I would grow up and get married that my dad and mother, whom I loved very dearly, would ever come and live with me. And it just doesn't work and I think that people here have found that out. And we like to go and visit. They come and visit us. We enjoy one another that way and don't get on one another's nerves. I don't think God ever created two families that could live together.

Apart from formal or informal travel of the one-day or weekend excursion type there is the camper-boating group. A number of Fun City residents own trailers and campers. These residents tour parts of the country for as little as a few days or as much as an entire summer. Parking campers, trailers, or boats upon one's property is not allowed. They are stored in a separate compound on the edge of town, designed specifically for that purpose. A storage area of this kind serves to keep the town neat and tidy. It is no overstatement to say that "Cleanliness is next to godliness" is an adage that is foremost in the minds of Fun City residents. The camper-trailer-boating compound is only one of many ways in which this preoccupation expresses itself.

Finally, there are the independently wealthy, many of whom belong to the Travel Club and arrange their trips through the club's agents. While Fun City generally offers a relatively healthy, warm, dry, smog-free climate, the summers (especially the days) are usually uncomfortably hot. Winters are, for some, too cool. Many residents who can afford it sublet during these periods, and go elsewhere for the climate or a change of scene. Some also come and go for varying periods of time throughout the year. Such residents leave for foreign countries for as much as three to six months at a time. In fact, many of these seasoned travelers and long-standing residents (a small percentage of the total population), while formally residing in Fun City, are really only occasional inhabitants. For them Fun City is a kind of home base for international touring. Indeed, some of the long-term residents only live there on weekends.

There are also one- or two-week trips to national parks, Canada, or Mexico. Apart from the camper-boater group, these vacations are frequently undertaken with the assistance of the Travel Club agent.

The above forms of travel, in conjunction with the one mentioned earlier regarding those active in sports, represent the different ways in which segments of Fun City residents occasionally "get away from it all."

In summary, it can be said that one-day excursions in one form or another (planned or individually initiated) are the most popular form of travel. While the independently wealthy frequently leave Fun City for long periods of time, other less affluent residents tour the country in campers for a few weeks at a time, primarily in search of the great outdoors. Notwithstanding the wanderlust of some Fun City residents, most Travel Club members restrict themselves to one-day excursions, while others hold only paper memberships. Some nonmembers, on the other hand, travel a great deal without the Travel Club's assistance. Finally, many residents live in Fun City the year round and rarely leave their homes.

A NOTE ON INTRACITY TRAVEL

The remark about persons rarely leaving their homes is not intended figuratively. It is very hot in Fun City a good part of the year and most residents are, because of age or illness, incapable of walking to the shopping center or Town Hall area, if they are more than a couple of blocks away. Residents rely heavily upon the use of their automobiles and golf carts for transportation. In fact, they must; there is no public transportation in Fun City. This constitutes a hardship for many residents who do not have automobiles. They must rely upon the generosity of neighbors (which tends to wear thin quickly) for intra- and intercity transportation. Neighbors are not always available or inclined to provide transportation to those who never learned to drive or are now unable to, even when they are reimbursed, as they usually are. For these persons the lack of public transportation within Fun City, or of connecting routes to adjacent towns, has resulted in their becoming "shut-ins." One resident put it this way: "I don't drive, you're dependent on your neighbors and that's not a very nice feeling. . . . There's no complaints about anything outside transportation. That's what they need badly." Notwithstanding her attempt to present a very positive picture of Fun City (she wept in the process), she did in fact complain about a number of other things.

Having one's own transportation is so important a feature of Fun City living that many residents who do not possess a valid drivers license drive their cars anyway. Many licenses have been revoked because of age, poor eyesight, or other physical handicaps. However, not driving in Fun City means not socializing, and becoming a social isolate before one's time. One can not go shopping or informally socialize at the Shopping Center and it is difficult to partake of formal social activities as well. In fact, being unable to drive is grounds for many leaving Fun City and moving closer to relatives and/or public transportation.

Most residents who own and operate a motor vehicle without a license usually stay within the confines of Fun City. Many are afraid to drive the freeways to other towns. Others (even those with valid licenses) refuse to drive at night because of failing eyesight. One resident notes: "There's so many people here that have cars that even have no license to drive them. They're all older people. They have to be a certain age when you come in [first become a resident of Fun City] and that transportation means quite a bit. . . ." Many residents did not anticipate the effects of a lack of public transportation on their life style, in that they were younger and healthier upon arrival and able to drive. Not being able to drive had simply not occurred to them. This condition affects many residents, as the average stay of Fun City residents is appreciable, judging from notations in the obituary columns and accounts of the residents. A surprising number seem to have been founding fathers. Most of the others had been there for three to five years. The effects of time upon one's health in old age can be dramatic and traumatic. One resident gave this account:

> *Mrs. B.*: When we moved out here (six years ago) we were the first ones on this block. And at that time there was only one widow in this whole block and now there are seven of us right in a row. I don't know, I think this is a bad side of the street. They're all on this side of the street. The other side of the street seems to be all right.
> *Mrs. F.*: No.
> *Mrs. B.*: Well, there's one widow over there.
> *Mrs. F.*: No, they lost three over there.

An unusual letter to the editor of the *Fun City News* (unusual in that letters to the editor are usually phrased so as not to give offense) notes that about 25 percent of all residents have no means of transportation. I believe her opening description of the effect of this situation is an accurate one.

> I walk through the streets and there is no sign of life. I see women with heavy bundles trudging up the road from the shopping center and wonder how much longer they can take it
> The Civic Association discusses everything but transportation. There is a taxi service but how many can pay seventy-five cents to town?
> The first two presidents of the Civic Association were farsighted men. They knew when the developer would move out, the Civic Association would have to take over. They were working toward that day. They gave their time and energy for all the people—not just one club.
> If money can be spent on repairs for the lawn bowling, shuffleboard courts and closed-circuit television, some should be spent on humanity.
> I understand there are fifteen hundred persons without transportation in Fun City. The people without transportation have two alternatives—move into an apartment that costs more, or into the new Fun City Garden apartments where prices are more than most people can pay. (Or leave Fun City.)
> Transportation was guaranteed when people signed the papers. It was in the literature also. The people were told not to worry, "It would be taken care of." People bought on the premise. Americans are independent people. No one wants to depend upon his neighbor. No neighbor wants others depending on him. Everyone wants to be free.

A NOTE ON THE PASSIVE WAY OF LIFE

An estimate by one informant, a mailman who has been on the route for six years, is that approximately 25 percent of Fun City's residents "never leave their homes." Many of these (and other more active) residents subscribe to "junk mail" listings in order to be able to receive and read some mail every day. "Mail call" for many residents has the same connotation that it has for those in other "total institutional" settings (such as the army or prison), it represents a significant part of one's everyday life. Apart from subscribing to "junk mail," there are other ways to ensure regular mail deliveries and establish ties with the outside world. Residents sometimes purchase two shares of this stock and three of that, in order to liven up the mail picture and have something to look forward to in the way of quarterly dividend checks and other critical business notices. The fact that one receives a check for $2.83 at the end of a business quarter is of no great moment. The fact that one receives a check is. Another source of mail, in this case the receipt of packages, is drug deliveries. Many—in fact most—Fun City residents belong to the American Association of Retired People. This means not only that one receives the association's newsletter, but also that one is entitled to a discount on drug purchases that is, according to one informant's estimate, approximately 15 percent.

> *Dr. J.:* Well, do a lot of people get their drugs through the A. A. R. P.?
> *Mr. K.:* Oh yes, ninety percent of the people in Fun City.
> *Mrs. K.:* Being a postman he knows that because he carries it to the homes.
> *Mr. K.:* We get a number two sack [mail sack] full of pills every morning [at the post office for delivery]. That's what we call it, "the pills" . . . but they're not maternity pills.

The volume of this particular delivery (a # 2 mailsack full daily) gives some indication of the extent of illness and/or hypochondria among Fun City residents.

An apt summary of the passive life style of most Fun City residents is provided by the maintenance chief.

> *Mr. X.:* I have children, old couple live next door to me, young couple next . . . I like that community you know. If I'm sixty-two or sixty-five I wouldn't live in it [Fun City]. . . . But there's other people who love it. . . . And that's why they have a community. They like to live in a community like this, good luck to them. And if you don't like it, you live somewhere else. . . . Well, I talk to a lot of people here. Some like it, some love it, some move out, and they . . . it's difficult. Like I have friends living here . . . worked yesterday . . . tenants in my building. I was managing a building in Parkville. They gave me the idea to move to this area. They said it was nice. They lived in Fun City six years, but they only come on the weekend. He's a big shot at an aerospace firm and they love it here. But I said you people don't live here seven days a week. You only live here two days out of the week. . . . Yeah, it's a very nice place, only people has to help a little bit more . . . there's a lot of lonesome people here . . . very lonesome. I see some gentlemen here every day . . . They walk along, light a cigarette . . . like lost sheep . . . If they organize a little more. Well it's difficult, you see . . . I was in Europe four years, in the states eight years. The people are nice here, but there's no sociable attitude . . . You know you go into a cafe and come in and join in and have a can of beer . . . I'm not a drinker . . . but it's so friendly. You don't have that here. You know everybody's afraid of his neighbor . . . Most of them stay home, watch T.V. I told them you should come out here. Have a good time. It's a million-dollar facility. It's all here for them. Use it more. It's all the same people I see around here. Very few new faces.

DEALING WITH DEATH

In a setting of this kind where age, inactivity, and poor health are prevalent, one soon comes to reflect upon death. While members of the larger community must also learn to live with death, it is a task that requires a particularly high level of adaptability in a retirement setting. The residents, their spouses, or friends are likely to be stricken at any time. One ardent golfer told of how he recently went out for a round of golf with a friend who fell dead in his presence on the golf course. While he had not personally witnessed an event of this kind before, he knew of many who had. How do residents deal with the inevitable, frequently imminent, prospect of death? Generally, the coping mechanism incorporates a combination of resignation and what the larger community would probably consider a macabre sense of humor toward serious illness and death.

Dr. J.: Is it [death] a topic of conversation among yourselves?

Mr. N.: No, we don't talk about it. It will talk for itself . . . I look at people down here, there have been some really big shots, big executives and stuff like that, but I feel like that . . . I remember Hollywood. I went out there in the early days when the motion picture industry was in its infancy. And the stage people from New York, you know, they would come out and kind of highbrow the people who were trying to make a living in the motion pictures. They were trying to get into it, you know. They would figure that they were a nobody. And "I was on the New York stage. And I'm so and so." And we had a saying out there: "You may have been bred in old Kentucky, but you're nothing but a crumb out here." That's the way I feel about all of us out here. We may have been so and so, but here, everybody, we're just nothing. . . .

Dr. J.: It's a kind of a morbid subject but do you get used to the idea [of people dying] or . . .

Mr. N.: Well, you have to.

Dr. J.: You have to?

Mr. N.: You bet ya. You have no choice. I've got to face that I'm not going to be here too long. I'm seventy-nine years of age. And God, how much longer can I live? A lot of my friends are that, some of them are older. Like around here there used to be an old actor. He used to be on the old steamboat on the Mississippi there. He used to go up and down there. He is quite an artist. He's about eighty-seven. And he's enjoying life here, you know. And we've got fellas like the Banana King here. He's worth millions. And he has all those banana plantations, what is it, down in one of those countries south of Mexico there. And uh, we've got a lot of very well-to-do people in here. And uh, but they're not going to live too long. You take, well, five years from now, gosh, it will make a big toll on the people that live here, you know. *Because all that you have here is the past. There is no future.* [Emphasis added.]

4/The residents: A demographic and political profile

I have presented in the first three chapters a description of Fun City, its facilities, planned and spontaneous social events, a discussion of the residents' participation in these events, or lack of it, the nature of interactions and interactional settings among the more active (and passive) residents, and, finally, the way they deal with poor health and the prospect of death. In this chapter, I will deal with the question of who the residents are, their former employment and place of origin, their political orientations, and finally their reasons for coming to Fun City.

ETHNIC MAKEUP

What is the ethnic makeup of Fun City? The easiest answer to this question is had by glancing at the following table compiled from 1970 census data:

Total Population	5,519
White population	5,516
Negro population	0
Indian population	0
Other specified races	2
Reported other races	1

It is easy to see from this data that to all intents and purposes there are no ethnic minorities in Fun City. The question arises, why not? There seems to be nothing to prevent it. The introduction to the *Fun City Householder's Directory* states:

> . . . Sales are restricted to persons over 50 (either partner) without school age children. In the present population of [Fun City] are people from every walk of life and all of the 50 United States plus 14 other countries.
>
> Living in [Fun City] homes and apartments are retired carpenters, plumbers, salesmen, sergeants, generals, janitors, corporation executives, inventors, teachers, doctors, lawyers, union officials, contractors, nurses, painters, artists, scientists, technicians, manufacturers, farmers, ranchers—a complete cross section of Americana.

Conspicuously absent from this "complete cross section of Americana" are Blacks, Indians, Chicanos, Japanese, Chinese, and, in fact, anyone not from white "middle America."

PROPERTY VALUES

How is this vast segment of the population informally excluded, or alternatively, why do they refuse to come to Fun City? Perhaps they are "priced out of the market." Are the prices of homes (or rental units) in Fun City prohibitive for these economically disadvantaged groups? The following table, again based upon 1970 census data, would indicate otherwise. While economically disadvantaged groups might be excluded from buying homes in the twenty- to sixty-thousand-dollar range, they would not be excluded from those in the five- to nineteen-thousand-dollar category. Indeed, many older blacks have managed to purchase homes in that price range in neighboring towns.

Rent of renter-occupied units		*Value of owner-occupied units*	
Less than $ 40	6	Less than $ 5,000	0
40–59	0	5,000–9,999	1
60–79	1	10,000–14,999	99
80–99	3	15,000–19,999	845
100–119	6	20,000–24,999	938
120–149	11	25,000–34,999	564
150–199	34	35,000–49,999	68
200–299	5	50,000 and up	2
300 and up	2		

Finally, homes in these price ranges would certainly not be prohibitive to "the black bourgeoisie" found in the large metropolitan area nearby from which most Fun City residents are recruited.

FORMER OCCUPATION

These data lead one to wonder about the former occupations of Fun City residents. Perhaps there is a selective recruitment operating, based upon former occupation and the general pursuit of "consciousness of kind." However, the directory tells us that the residents come from a wide spectrum of occupations, ranging from janitors to corporation executives. This may be true when taken literally but *how many* janitors, how many generals and corporation executives reside in Fun City? Perhaps there is a common denominator to these occupations that is not obvious at the outset. An analysis of the material found in the *Fun City Householder's Directory*, listing the homeowner, his address, phone number, and former occupation, reveals that while there are hundreds of retired professionals, independent business owners, salesmen, civil servants, and retired military personnel, one can count the number of janitors in Fun City on one hand. Indeed, there are very few residents who come from the ranks of unskilled labor.

Out of a total of approximately 3300 entries in the directory, 1828 are sufficiently unambiguous to allow for their coding into ten occupational categories. By ambiguous listings, I mean such entries as "Union Pacific," "Pacific Telephone Co.," or "Douglas Aircraft." One cannot discern the nature of the occupation that the resident held in the above settings from such abbreviated descriptions.

While many others were listed by name, residence and phone number, their former occupations were excluded entirely. Table 1 summarizes those entries that allow for coding, using occupational categories that emerge naturally from the data.

Basically, these data lend further support to the contention that Fun City residents do not represent a "cross section of Americana." Not only are ethnic minorities excluded from the population, but there are very few "poor whites." The vast majority of Fun City residents are professionals, white collar workers, skilled blue collar workers, or retired military personnel. Less than 4 percent of all Fun City residents were recruited from the ranks of unskilled labor. The case could be made, in fact, that the resident's former occupation was a class factor contributing to the exclusion of blacks, ethnic minorities, and poor whites from the city.

A selective factor based upon "consciousness of kind" was clearly operating in the case of Fun City residents. Indeed, this was publicly acknowledged by the City Manager in an article intended to rebut Ralph Nader's position on retirement communities such as Fun City. The segregation one finds in Fun City (by age, occupation, income, and race) is taken to be perfectly "natural" and a result of "natural gravitation." How one squares this position with the policy statement noted in the *Fun City Householder's Directory* that residents represent "a complete cross-section of Americana" is difficult to fathom.

The Fun City Manager, a featured speaker at a recent university seminar on aging, disagreed with Ralph Nader, one of the other speakers, who thought that Fun City's segregation by age was as bad as segregation by race or religion.

The manager summarized Ralph Nader's talk for the Civic Association Board and concluded:

I disagree with him [Nader] in the utmost when he, in his address before the assembled greats of the retirement and aging specialists, stated that retirement communities were wrong and against nature, so to speak.

TABLE 1   FORMER OCCUPATIONS OF FUN CITY RESIDENTS
PRIOR TO RETIREMENT

1.	Professionals (combining five categories)	544
2.	Independent business owners	351
3.	Skilled labor	260
4.	Salesmen	174
5.	Civil servants	158
6.	Military	117
7.	Real estate brokers	70
8.	Unskilled labor	69
9.	"Managers"	47
10.	Farmers and ranchers	38
	TOTAL	1828

When former occupations were given for both husband and wife, only the husband's occupation was considered. Where there was only one resident per household, his or her former occupation was included.

"Housewife" has not been included as an occupational category even though 95 of Fun City's residents listed their former (and present) occupation as such.

He stated that they were causing and furthering segregation.

I disagree with Ralph Nader violently, not with the segregation angle—because that is true—just as priests congregate, women congregate at bridge games, men move towards sporting events, men and women dance; there is a natural gravitation—but rather, I disagree with him when he says that this segregation is bad.

What is bad with a community where there are shared the ideas, the same attitudes, the same feelings regarding all aspects of life?

After all, don't we all—the young and the old—tend to get together according to age, color, and beliefs? Is it so bad to wish to spend the last, and possibly the best years of our lives with those who agree with us?

This, in essence, was my point at the meeting. I hope you approve.

FORMER PLACE OF RESIDENCE

Another approach to the problem would be to ask, from what parts of the county are Fun City residents recruited? Perhaps they come from sectors of the county in which blacks are few. The Table 2 gives a breakdown (obtained from the *Fun City Householder's Directory*) of the former place of origin of Fun City residents.

TABLE 2   DISTRIBUTION OF PLACE OF ORIGIN OF FUN CITY
RESIDENTS BY STATE AND COUNTRY

Alabama	3	Louisiana	3	Ohio	83
Alaska	2	Maryland	7	Oklahoma	5
Arizona	20	Maine	1	Oregon	27
Arkansas	1	Massachusetts	10	Pennsylvania	37
California	1714	Michigan	82	Rhode Island	2
Colorado	41	Minnesota	55	South Carolina	0
Connecticut	15	Mississippi	0	South Dakota	4
Delaware	1	Missouri	24	Tennessee	1
Florida	14	Montana	17	Texas	11
Georgia	2	Nebraska	17	Utah	17
Hawaii	6	Nevada	9	Vermont	1
Idaho	6	New Hampshire	1	Virginia	8
Illinois	196	New Jersey	27	Washington	42
Indiana	30	New Mexico	5	West Virginia	1
Iowa	40	New York	63	Wisconsin	43
Kansas	15	North Carolina	2	Wyoming	8
Kentucky	2	North Dakota	12	Washington, D.C.	8
				Origins Unknown	215

Australia	1	Japan	1
Canada	12	Mexico	1
Egypt	1	Saudi Arabia	1
England	1	Switzerland	1

IMPLICATIONS OF THE DATA

First, there are more Fun City residents from California than from all the other states combined. While blacks constitute only 11.2 percent of the United States population, they represent 18 percent of the population of the metropolitan center from which most Fun City residents were recruited. In addition, the population of the metropolis includes 8 percent Mexican Americans, 10 percent Jewish, and 3 percent Orientals (Maullin, 1971: 41).

It is interesting to note as well, how one may easily be deceived by the notation cited earlier in the *Householder's Directory* regarding the diversity of Fun City residents: "'In the present population of [Fun City] are people form every walk of life and all of the 50 United States plus 14 other countries."

Judging from the entries in the *Householder's Directory*, only 8 other countries are represented, but more important is the fact that only one person represents seven out of eight of these countries. Only Canada has as many as a dozen. Such "cross cultural" influences as exist in Fun City can only constitute what is generally referred to as "token integration," undertaken on behalf of public relations. Indeed, the statement that there are representatives from all the 50 states is misleading, as can be seen from the entries for Mississippi and South Carolina. Apart from California most residents seem to come from the Northeast and Midwest.

In summary, the notion that blacks and other ethnic minorities do not reside in Fun City's major recruitment area must also be discarded.

COMPOSITION OF HOUSEHOLDS

Another indicator of who lives in Fun City can be had from an analysis of the *Householder's Directory* with respect to household occupancy. Table 3 is informative.

TABLE 3   SEX COMPOSITION OF FUN CITY HOUSEHOLDS

Sex composition	Number of households
1 male, 1 female	2238
1 female	504
1 male	166
2 females	19
2 males	7
[a]2 females, 1 male	10
1 female, 2 males	4
3 females	3
[b]Single person, sex unknown	40
1 female, 1 son attending college	1
	2992

[a] One of the households was composed of a parent couple and their daughter, who was attending college.

[b] Could not determine sex of occupant because of insufficient information given in guide.

The data indicate that by far the majority of Fun City households are composed of one male and one female (2238 out of 2992). However, one ought not to assume that these were, in every case, married couples. They were not. There were certain economic advantages (and some social) especially for the men, in "shacking up." Such informal living arrangements were acknowledged by some residents but it could not be established how widespread a practice this was.

Another interesting aspect is the number of single males compared to single females. The latter outnumber the former by slightly more than three to one. One might expect there would be a considerable interest among the members of this set in remarrying. Indeed, residents frequently mentioned that a considerable number of remarriages between residents had taken place within Fun City. This claim prompted a search of the county records, and I was surprised to find that only ten Fun City residents had been married within the county between December 30, 1970, and November 11, 1971. The average age of the males was seventy-three; of females, sixty-six. The residents' perception of the number of residents remarrying (as in the case of the number participating in formal club activities) seems to have been greatly exaggerated. Indeed, while the exact number remains unknown, it is a fair guess that many widowers and widows prefer more informal living arrangements for living together.

GENTEEL DISCRIMINATION

What is the effect of an all-white middle and upper class population on the black (or poor white) prospective buyer considering Fun City as a place to retire? The message begins with the real estate broker, who gladly shows prospective buyers, whoever they are, available properties. However, the message for blacks and ethnics, while it is subtle, is unambiguous. It sounds something like this: "We would be happy to sell you a home in Fun City but we really think that you would be happier elsewhere." The potential buyer, on seeing who his neighbors are and the reception he receives in public places, (the shopping center and Town Hall areas) where heads still turn to see blacks (or not completely respectable-looking whites) can only agree with the realtor's assessment. While there is nothing on paper to prevent one from buying a home and retiring in Fun City, only a masochistic black or member of another ethnic minority would do so.

An example of the strong binding effects of "tacit understandings" on Fun City residents, with respect to excluding poor whites (and blacks of any economic level), was revealed to me at the conclusion of a home interview. I was about to leave when my informants suggested that we visit another Fun City resident, a friend of theirs who lived across town. On the way to the car I commented on the casual (and unusual) attitude of their neighbor toward mowing the lawn. The lawn was uncut and untrimmed, and weeds grew everywhere. The house also had a "do it yourself" paint job that gave the entire property an incongruous look, with respect both to the adjacent homes and to the community at large. This casual comment elicited the following story. The neighbor was in the hospital and unable to care for his property. He would probably not return to his home, but because of his age and illness would be placed in a nursing home. Furthermore, he was on "welfare," one of 13 Fun City residents in that predicament.

When my informants first came to Fun City four years ago, they believed the property they purchased to be a very attractive business deal. It offered a well-built house on a large corner lot, in a good section of town, and at a very reasonable price. They later learned that the property had been up for sale for two years with no takers. The reason: It was adjacent to the neighbor on welfare. Upon moving into their new home, they also found that no one on their block (indeed in the neighborhood) would speak to them. They have made friends since then, but their best friends are a couple they knew before moving to Fun City, who bought a home there soon after my informants arrived (a fairly frequent Fun City recruitment pattern). Other, more casual acquaintances (and they are a socially active couple) were not found on their block or in their neighborhood. They had to make a conscious effort to establish friendships elsewhere across town.

One resident who was unusually candid in describing Fun City facades had this to say of the dozen or so welfare recipients in town.

> There are some poor citizens . . . who make it with the help of food stamps and just manage on their social security. But if that is so, it's considered shameful, and they sneak into [Jonesville] or Missiontown to do their shopping so that the food stamps are not seen [by other Fun City residents]. . . . They will go to some lengths to make sure that their checks [welfare checks] are cashed elsewhere.

Some indication of the residents' cautious attitude toward discussing the question of blacks, ethnics or poor whites as potential neighbors can be had from the following:

Mrs. B.: Oh, they're [Fun City residents] from every walk of life.
Dr. J.: Are there any black families in Fun City?
Mrs. F.: Oh, a couple of black families live here.
Mrs. B.: Oh, I've never seen'em.
Mrs. F.: There's two black families living here.
Mrs. B.: I know there's a Mexican family.
Mrs. F.: Well, there's a Mexican family, an Indian family, there's two black families I know [that live here].
Mrs. B.: But as far as Negroes, I've never seen them, of course.
Mrs. F.: The Shoemakers live here and then there's another black family that live here.
Mrs. B.: Does he live here? I thought he lived over in [Jonesville]?
Mrs. F.: No, they live here, two black families.
Dr. J.: Why do you think that more blacks haven't moved to Fun City?
Mrs. B.: It probably just isn't attractive to 'em. I don't know. As far as I know there is nothing against it.
Mrs. B.: It's just their own choice.
Mrs. F.: Well, [Jonesville] has an awful big colored section and they like to be with their own.
Mrs. F.: And they can live cheaper over there I think.
Dr. J.: So any blacks seem to congregate over in [Jonesville], you think?
Mrs. B.: Well, of course they've always been over there.
Mrs. B.: Yeah.
Mrs. F.: And there's a lot of Mexican people over there too, you know.
Mrs. B.: But then of course you'll find the Mexican people scattered all through

this part of the country, you know, and the colored too. But around Jonesville it's just really concentrated.

Mrs. F.: Listen, they're happy among their own people, why shouldn't they stay there? Nobody bothers them and . . .

Mrs. F.: You don't have to dislike 'em, but they're happier with their own people, their own churches are there.

Dr. J.: I see.

Mrs. F.: But there's two colored families. You didn't know they were living here?

Mrs. B.: I didn't know they lived in Fun City. I thought they lived in Jonesville.

Mrs. F.: And there's a colored man married to a white woman here too.

Mrs. B.: Gee, you get around more than I do. [Laugh]

Mrs. F.: Well, I got that information from Mrs. J.

There are, of course, other possible explanations for why blacks and ethnics are not found in Fun City than those given above. One found in the literature holds that blacks growing old are retained for longer periods within the extended family. This account is subject to the following critique. Adjacent to Fun City is the small town (and rural ghetto) of Jonesville, previously noted, which has experienced within the last few years the unusual effects of a reversed migration: poor blacks moving there from an adjacent urban ghetto. Many of these recent immigrants are older individuals who are not a part of extended families. Then too, the older middle-class black, who would, economically speaking, be more likely to move to Fun City, is (like his white counterpart) less likely to remain a part of an extended family than is a poor black. The notion that there are no blacks with sufficient incomes or initial inclinations to become Fun City residents is, I believe, difficult to maintain.

SELF-DEFENSES

How do residents feel about their all-white middle class community? For example, do they harbor feelings of guilt or "bad faith"? It seems not. Part of the reciprocal defense residents have against feelings of bigotry, or guilt, has to do with the general organization of communications and interactions in Fun City. An over-riding concern among Fun City residents (noted earlier in the work) is not to offend others. It is felt that this is best accomplished by not bringing up potentially disruptive topics, such as religion, race, and politics. In a symbolic sense, it was the indiscriminate extension of "good fences make good neighbors" that relegated most Fun City conversation to "safe" inanities.

While the reciprocal and widespread application of this informal norm helped to ensure one neither gave nor took offense, it also led to inconsequential "gray on gray" forms of interactions that did little to promote meaning or a zest for life among the residents. On the surface it seemed that "consideration for the feelings of others makes everyone get along" 'was both an altruistic sentiment and sound social policy. Translated into behavioral terms, however, it meant that one either withdrew from the social arena in self-defense or restricted one's interactions to uncontroversial and inconsequential forms of encounters. For the most part topics of conversation centered around what one would have for dinner, gardening, a forthcoming card game, or for the more active member, some upcoming social club activity. Nor do I mean to imply that this policy succeeded in creating by default a feeling of brotherhood or good will among the residents. It did not. There was in fact within formal club memberships (some clubs more than others) and other informal groupings, plentiful backbiting. This was especially true in the former and resulted in many "low key" or ailing residents, who had no stomach for conflict or the game of "one-upmanship," dropping out. These included not only residents whose prior social life could be characterized as reserved, but those with formerly active social lives.

WHY FUN CITY?

Having considered the question of who lives in Fun City and some of the ways in which residents maintain the current racial and economic balance (or imbalance), let us now consider why residents chose Fun City in the first place. Why Fun City and not one of the many adjacent retirement communities or those rapidly springing up in other areas of the country? Upon direct presentation of the question "How did you come to settle in Fun City?" the answer always seemed to include the following features: (1) it's safe in the streets (there are no blacks, ethnics, drug addicts, hippies, or other "undesirables" in Fun City); (2) it's healthy (warm, dry and relatively smog-free); (3) it's uncongested (no traffic jams); (4) there's plenty to do (clubs and scheduled activities); (5) it's well-situated geographically (fairly convenient to beaches, mountains, and desert).

On considering this list, and in light of my observations and the accounts of the residents themselves, it is difficult to understand why they found the above to be desirable features of Fun City living. Let us consider the items in this list and the ways in which they applied to the residents' life style, one at a time.

"It's Safe in the Streets"

Granted many came to Fun City from the metropolitan center or other urban settings where it is not always safe in the streets, especially for older people. Of course, they often came from respectable or "better" residential sections of towns where it was relatively safe. However, it should be allowed that one's perception of the degree of safety (for either person or property) tends to decline with age and one's own ability to cope. That a person is "not what he used to be" is true in more ways than one with regard to the effects of age upon the self. One woman put it this way: "Today with so much violence, some of the people have come out here almost in self-defense. . . . We know the problems of the city and it's dangerous for older people to be there alone."

It would be understandable that residents were concerned for their safety in the metropolis and that they came to Fun City because it was "safe in the streets" if it were not for the fact that Fun City residents never use the streets. You can drive through Fun City on any day and at any time and not see a dozen people out walking. All the streets are lined on both sides with wide, well-kept sidewalks. The objection may be raised that it is frequently too hot in Fun City for walking. This was not true in the mornings or evenings. Some residents (very few) did take a morning walk. Scarcely anyone took an evening walk. The question arises, why not? It is cool and pleasant in the evening. The answer from many residents was, "It's safe in the streets in Fun City but not so safe that I would walk at night."

In fact it is difficult to assess how safe it really is. As noted earlier, the streets are deserted and there is little to bring the outsider to Fun City. On the other hand, should one come to Fun City to commit crimes against property or person, there is little to prevent it. Fun City has no police force. The State Highway Patrol cruises through town a couple of times a day, but apart from that there is nothing but Fun City's isolation and lack of attractions to make it "safe in the streets." It is noteworthy that though there seems to be little crime against persons, burglaries are reported from time to time in the *Fun City News*, and residents have related others that went unreported. The extent of the underreporting of crimes against persons and property is difficult to estimate. I feel that it is probably not extensive, but exceeds what residents believe it to be. The following fairly well summarizes the average resident's opinion of Fun City security.

Well, like every place, it's got its good points and its bad points. And, uh, if I knew any better place to go I'd go there. But the way things are nowadays you don't have much of a choice any more. It's still safe around here. You can walk the streets at night. You can go away and lock your house up, and it's a comfortable feeling when you come back . . .

It is generally true that things will be there upon their return. However, sometimes things are missing. One resident related the following:

The people next door own the hardware and gift shop here, and the lady [the neighbor] happened to be at the window and saw they [the absent residents] had a light burning like you're supposed to, and she saw two fellows carrying what seemed like a big box around the back way. Well, there's nothing to getting in you know. All they had to do was slit the screen. And they drove a car up, put this box in and away they went. Well, they took that and went through all the drawers but no jewelry. (I guess they were looking for money.) And they took this beautiful stereophonic, you know radio and everything, and all the records. And Joan [the woman whose house was burglarized] said, "Are they going to be surprised when they put that first record on." It was "How Great Thou Art," more on the religious you know than that bebop stuff. And they also took a clock radio that their kids had just given them for Christmas.

In short, "safe in the streets" is a peculiar notion for Fun City. First because there is no police force to help make the community safe (it has to rely upon its isolation for that) and second because the residents really do not possess the feeling of security they claimed brought them there. They lock their houses and leave a light burning upon departing (indeed, they keep both screen door and main door locked even when they are at home) and are very leery of walking in the streets at night. Apart from the above is the fact that residents are simply not found in the streets of Fun City even in broad daylight. This was true even during the cooler parts of day, or on cool overcast days. It is peculiar then, that residents would make so much of "law and order" in Fun City when it seems to be a notion, not only of questionable validity, but also having so little influence upon their everyday life.

The questionable validity of the statement "It's safe in the streets" can be understood from a note in the *Fun City News* by the police captain in the Sheriff's Department responsible for patrolling Fun City and the surrounding areas.

> Fun City is the safest community so far as crime is concerned among all of the cities under jurisdiction of the Sheriff's substation, [the] Captain told the *News* this week.
>
> This despite the fact that there has been a recent rash of burglary crime and an attempted mugging here.
>
> [The] Captain said his office has taken all of the necessary steps for patrol protection of Fun City, plus other measures to curb such offenses.

"It's Healthy"

What of the second condition that residents almost always mention as influencing their choice of Fun City: "It's healthy." Fun City does have a warm, dry, and relatively smog-free climate that is good for some of the common ailments of old age, such as rheumatism and arthritis. However it is frequently very hot in Fun City. This results in two conditions that are not beneficial to the residents' health. First, because of the heat, all of Fun City's facilities, the Town Hall and shopping center areas, are air conditioned. For many this has a kind of boomerang effect. Residents who have sought Fun City's climate because of its salubrious effects upon their rheumatism or arthritis, cannot avail themselves of the social and recreational facilities because of the untoward effects of the air conditioning upon their physical complaints. As a result they spend most of their time at home, or outside in shaded areas, which restricts their movements and social life considerably. Many people can not participate in formal club activities because of the air conditioning. For those not troubled by it there is the problem of getting from their homes to Fun City's two main areas of social life. As was pointed out earlier, many do not drive and there is no public transportation. If not for the heat, some might have walked, but because of the "healthy climate"' they have become essentially "shut-ins." Then too, while hot, dry climates are good for providing symptom relief from some of the ailments that frequently accompany old age, the long-standing effects of the sun and heat upon the health of the general populace is questionable. A more temperate climate might have been healthier.

Quite apart from the question of climate, any consideration of whether a potential retirement setting is healthy or not needs to include a discussion of medical care facilities, their quality and availability. In this crucial regard Fun City is sorely lacking. There are no major medical facilities located in Fun City. A hospital planned for construction in Fun City some years ago has never materialized. There is only out-patient service available at the Fun City Medical Clinic. Most of Fun City's four doctors, two dentists, two optometrists, and one chiropractor are located in this facility. Some are situated in the shopping center complex. None of the doctors will accept new patients even for out-patient treatment since they are all overworked. The result for new residents is that they need to seek all medical assistance elsewhere. Established residents may receive out-patient treatment for chronic complaints at the clinic. All acute and emergency cases must be treated elsewhere. Waiting to be driven by the Fun City's ambulance service (for an annual fee of $30) to a facility up to 30 miles away can be especially damaging to someone suffering a heart attack or other serious physical complaint requiring immediate medical attention.

Not only is medical service almost unavailable inside Fun City; it has limited availability on the outside as well. There are three major medical facilities in the larger cities within a radius of 30 miles. However, getting there and back for scheduled appointments is a great problem for many residents. It has already been noted that many do not drive. Some of those who drive do not drive the freeways, and some of those who drive the freeways do not drive at night. Not only does Fun City not have public transportation, but there is only one bus out of Fun City each morning that returns in the late afternoon. The bus does go to one of the three major medical facilities but the fact that it leaves and returns only once a day frequently excludes the possibility of scheduling appointments even at that facility. In short, major or even out-patient medical service is not readily available to residents who sorely need it.

"It's Uncongested"

There is no denying the fact that Fun City is uncongested. However, this can be considered a virtue by the potential newcomer only insofar as it promises to allow him greater freedom of movement than he found in an urban setting. The urbanite's argument goes something like this: "What good is all the cultural life and other virtues of city living if traffic is so congested that they become inaccessible." This is especially true in old age when one is reluctant to "fight traffic," drive the freeways, or drive at night. Fun City, while it has less to offer, has activities easily accessible. Once again, this is true only if you drive, are not troubled by the air conditioning, want to become an active member of a club (some of the hazards were previously outlined), or are interested in the available activities or club members. Many residents are excluded on one or more of these grounds.

"There's Plenty to Do"

Another attraction residents claimed to have drawn them to Fun City was "There's plenty to do." It was anticipated that one's leisure would not weigh heavily upon one, because there were so many scheduled activities to participate in. Residents always tell of the numerous clubs, how nice it is to have these activities available, and how many persons belong to one or another of them. The story always unfolds in such a way as to convince the listener that the person relating the story is an active participant himself. However when asked, "How many clubs do you belong to," it was almost always the case that respondents fitted into one of the following categories: (1) held memberships in no clubs; (2) held paper memberships in one or more clubs but participated in none; (3) held paper memberships in one or more but participated in only one; (4) held an active membership in only one.

In short, most residents are aware of the many formal activities available to them. Their perception is that their lack of participation is the exception, and that most people are actively involved in Fun City's formal social structure. As was demonstrated earlier, they are wrong. Only several hundred of Fun City's six thousand residents are actively engaged in club activities. Notwithstanding a large paper membership, most residents partake of a passive way of life. It is not only the residents who seem to misperceive the extent of social activity in Fun City. Newspaper reporters from outside, spending the day there for a human interest story, also overestimate the extent of the town's social life. This is easily done if one focuses on the Town Hall or Activity Center and Shopping Center areas, as most visitors do. Indeed, this is not surprising in that one naturally attends to interesting features of one's environment and ignores the trivia that constitute most of social life. This is especially true in Fun City, and especially true of reporters seeking to write a human interest story. Leave the Activity Center and for a journalist there is nothing interesting in Fun City to write about. While the many clubs and planned social activities (along with the other features I have noted) have influenced some to come to Fun City it is clear that few participate in them. It is certainly no explanation for why they remained.

"It's Well Situated"

Finally, there is the notion among Fun City residents that the community is "well situated"—it is near the desert, beaches, and mountains. This is true. One is within easy driving distance of a wide range of environmental settings. However, we must remember that many residents do not drive, and that others who drive are unable to drive the freeways that make these settings easily accessible. "Well situated" may have been an important feature of Fun City for the camper and boater set, who comprise a relatively small group of Fun City residents. But certainly, many residents who mentioned "It's well situated" as a reason for coming to Fun City have never been able or inclined to avail themselves of this asset.

The author is not trying to make the case that some of these features did not influence the decisions of some residents in choosing Fun City. I'm sure they did. However these features seem to play a small role in the everyday life of most residents. Once again, if they played any part in getting residents there, it is hard to see what part they played in keeping them there.

The "Real" Reasons

If the above factors were not instrumental in the residents choosing (and remaining in) Fun City, what was? The ways in which residents became committed to Fun City are varied. Some (who had not yet contemplated retirement) were on vacation and just stopped to look—long enough for an able real estate agent to sell them a lot "as a future investment." Those who bought lots as an investment did not dispose of them as an investment—that is, resell them at a profit. Rather, this maneuver was responsible for many in this category retiring sooner than they had anticipated, building on their lot, and moving to Fun City. The following is a fairly typical account:

Dr. J.: How long have you been in Fun City? About nine or ten years, wasn't it?

Mrs. Q.: Yes, about ten years. We heard about this place, we were visiting some friends that John [her husband] knew . . . who now live here by the way and they wanted us to come out and see this place. . . . I was teaching in Suburbia then. I taught there for nine years, and I said, "retirement communities," who the heck wants a bunch of old people around you. I said that's the last thing in the world I want but I'll go and visit them anyway. So we stayed at the Royal Inn and I was amazed. What first interested me was the fact that the homes were attractive and well built for the money that we could afford. So that was the interest and we knew that, or John felt, it was my idea that when he got to be sixty he ought to retire, or sixty-two I think it was. Of course it's always fine when somebody else is going to retire but when it's you, you think it's ridiculous. But I thought he had been in the government a long time. He was working and the hours were long, and horrible schedules and overtime and all that business. And I thought well, that rat race in Metropolis is just too much. So [he] better just retire. And so we just heard about this place [from a friend they were visiting while on vacation]. There was nothing here but field you know, just, it had been a little duck swamp and a little tiny house, so we went in and looked it over and I thought this will never be anything. Who ever wants to come here. So we put five hundred dollars down really for an investment. I though well you know if nothing else we can buy this and sell it.

Dr. J.: Sure.

Mrs. O.: Well, things began to get worse in Metropolis and we loved the countryside. It made me think a lot of my home on the prairie where I had grown up among the hills and so on, and so we went on with the deal.

Now that was in January of 'sixty-two, and January of 'sixty-three, the year following, we got our key for this house. And this was the largest of the first plans that they built. I decided to get the biggest there was, including the fireplace and double garage which they had just for a few weeks, and then my mother was going to live with us who passed away before we moved out here. So then we moved out here in June of 'sixty-three. But I continued to teach in Suburbia. And John decided he wasn't going to retire until the following Christmas because of his retirement age [he would get a larger retirement].

So I taught in the following year, although we'd sold our home in Suburbia and moved all our furniture [to Fun City]. We had an apartment right across from the school. You know that area, and I had a marvelous position, I just loved it and I hated to leave. . . . It was a challenging work and one I liked and we had a wonderful relationship with the staff and I was very active, at the top of my profession, when I had to make this decision. But what really [did it] was that I got sick and tired of driving out there to Fun City every weekend. Just murder.

Dr. J.: It's a long drive.

Mrs. O.: You know, ninety miles. And then coming out here and this place was always dusty. Cause that's when they didn't have any trees and it was a mess. So I just handed in my resignation and I decided, well I'll see what I can get out there [near Fun City].

She did find a job teaching near Fun City but retired soon after, "So I retired a little early, about three or four years before I would have to."

As previously noted, many mentioned coming to Fun City for health reasons.

Many of those who extolled the virtues of Fun City in terms of the points noted earlier, would often, as the interview wore on, admit that they would have preferred to live elsewhere (at another retirement setting or within the greater community) usually near the beach for the view, the temporate climate, and for the better social, medical, and shopping facilities. Frequently however, their health, or that of their spouse, did not permit it.

> *Dr. J.:* Did you try another setting before retiring to Fun City?
> *Mr. D.:* No, I looked over in X Beach. And uh, my wife had a little sinus trouble near the coast, and so she could not take it back there. But I think I always had an idea that I would retire in one of those apartments in Y Beach overlooking the ocean there. When I lived there (near Y Beach) I used to hike down there and up and down on the strand and go out on the pier in the evening. You know, and get my exercise. Think things over. You'd see judges [he was a lawyer] doing the same thing, and lawyers. And we'd sit there and shoot the bull on the benches overlooking the beautiful ocean. And I often thought I would like to have one of those apartments, big apartments, down there. And then look over the ocean and have your television. And I like the climate there. And uh, maybe you could get out and walk—people walk there at night. That's what they do on the strand there at night. Walk out on the pier and watch the fishermen. And us, it's very nice there. But, with my wife, its just too moist down there, that's all. So I had to look for a dry place. Well, where you going to find it except here? Because we went down to X Beach and looked at that. Of course, these others (retirement communities) down below there hadn't been started yet.

While health and happenstance (or a combination of both) brought many residents to Fun City, being close to children and grandchildren also figured prominently in their choice. Remember that the majority of residents came from within the state and most of these from nearby Metropolis. Many had long-standing friendships there. However, old friends died off, and there remained children and grandchildren as the last remaining link to the past.

Very often residents from out of state have moved to Fun City to be near their children, who are frequently settled in Metropolis, its suburbs, or other nearby towns. As I have pointed out, this does not always work out as well as they hoped. With the passage of time, residents see less and less of the children and grandchildren. For many, visits occur only on holidays or other special occasions. Then too, not all visits are welcomed ones. Children visiting their parents in Fun City sometimes have ulterior motives, such as borrowing money from parents for business or other needs. In the opinion of the residents this practice sometimes leads to feelings of resentment. In short, residents are ambivalent. They enjoy visitors but not for long. This was true even of grandchildren, for they make lots of noise, dirty the house, step on plants, and generally disturb (sometimes shatter) the peace and tranquillity of Fun City living. Notwithstanding their love for their grandchildren, this proves to be more than some residents can tolerate for more than a day at a time.

Many residents, in other words, are on the horns of a dilemma. They enjoy having friends and relatives visit, but they also enjoy the peace, quiet, and general low-key existence that Fun City offers. In brief, their ability to cope has been reduced considerably with age, and Fun City gives them (in some ways at least) little to cope with. The vivid imagery of one resident (cited later in this chapter) comes to mind. "This [Fun City] is a retreat. It's sort of a false paradise in a way. We're not of the world and yet do we want to be?"

Another factor drawing residents to Fun City, (and this was especially true of early residents) was that it offered good value in retirement settings near Metropolis, before the competition stiffened and inflation set in. While relatively inexpensive housing was important to those with lower level "fixed incomes," it was also appealing to independently wealthy persons. In the case of the latter one might well ask why. Some independently wealthy persons were as concerned (perhaps more concerned) about their future financial security on a fixed income than those who really had something to worry about. One resident, who has lost $100,000 on the stock market within the past few years, an amount that has reduced his "fixed income" by some $600 per month (a trifle given his holdings) had this to say:

> And uh, yesterday the market went down. It was something—today it is down to over two again. The money she's [his wife] lost—and she's nineteen years younger than I am. Of course, I'm a disabled vet—I don't have too much to worry about. She has it to live that long, with inflation coming. And she has no social security. She just has nothing. And I'm nineteen years older than she is, but if I should die tomorrow, why nineteen years from now, I don't know . . .

Later in the interview he went on to note:

> Well, I'll tell you: It's a reasonable place to live. Its a cheap place to live. Of course, the homes cost a lot more now than they did when I came here [10 years ago]. When I came here I paid $16,000 for three bedrooms, two baths, double carport, on the golf course, east–west exposure; so I can get the sun in the morning, and sit out there in the afternoon and watch the golfers. And I bought it on time because I could make more money investing than I could paying in cash. If I want to sell it, if I have a mortgage on it, it is a whole lot easier to sell than if I have to ask for cash or finance some way. And I paid as little down as possible. My interest is four and three quarters. And the guarantee brings it up to five and a quarter percent—I pay interest on a thirty-year loan. So, uh, it really makes me money with my income. Why, it gets my house down, because I can take that as an expense, the interest I pay, you know. And its mostly all interest I pay. The principle doesn't amount to much over thirty years. . . . So I'm living here at the cheapest rent. I figure it costs me for that home down there around seventy-five dollars a month. Where am I going to live in three bedrooms, fixed up like they are, built like they are, constructed like they are, on the golf course, and everything for seventy-five dollars a month? So I made a smart thing. Anyway, my house, if I wanted to sell it today, I could sell it for twice as much.

The above, while it seems to offer a reasonable account of why one might have come to Fun City ten years ago, is really less convincing than it seems. For example, ten years ago it was not situated on a golf course, but on "empty fields and a duck swamp." Why would an intelligent and highly paid professional choose to retire on a duck swamp, even allowing for the good financial terms? Since it was not a business venture (he did not rent or resell the property at a profit) why has he lived here these past 10 years? Furthermore, since he is still independently wealthy, why is he so concerned with financial security that he remains there? His reasons for doing so are not clear. It may be, at least in part, the same factors that make older persons seek "safety in the streets," "peace and quiet," and a move away from urban congestion. That is, a sense of financial insecurity (even among those who are financially secure) may be a part of the general insecurity that accompanies failing health and the general inability to cope. The search for financial security still operates as a consideration for many in choosing Fun City. Even now, allowing for inflation, Fun City gives the potential buyer fair value for his money. We have seen that middle and even upper income earners are concerned about living on a "fixed income" even when that income is fixed at a high level.

The question arises, in light of the considerations that brought residents to Fun City, why do they remain? For example, children move and the residents rarely see them or their grandchildren. The ailing spouse who was once responsible for their coming to a warm dry climate instead of the beach community they would have preferred, dies. They fall ill and require more medical attention than Fun City can provide, or than is readily accessible in adjacent communities. They are no longer able to drive and there is no public transportation in Fun City. In short, many of Fun City's more attractive features for potential homeowners become, with time, liabilities. In light of this and the economic independence of most Fun City residents why do they stay? The best single answer to this question seems to be inertia. Moving requires one sell his home, pack belongings, investigate preferable settings, find a new home there, and so on and so on. With increasing age and ailments one is no longer able to muster the energy a move requires. Then too, one is too old and infirm to enjoy the benefits of a move. If one could have retired to a preferred setting 10 years ago, it might have made a difference. However, it is of little consequence where you are now if you feel too old or too ill to enjoy the change. Moving also means leaving a familiar environment and life style for unknown and untried ones. Few older persons, particularly conservative, well-situated, white, middle-class persons, feel that adventuresome. Indeed that was why many chose Fun City in the first place.

POLITICS

Politics in Fun City offers a peculiar amalgam of political opinion. While it is true that, statistically speaking, Fun City is generally what it seems to be, a conservative white middle-class retirement community, this characterization does violence to any effort to be "true to the phenomena." Granting that right-wing Republicans outnumber Democrats by more than three to one, party affiliation is not always a good indicator of political opinion or behavior within or between political groupings. For example, two women, both of whom were Republicans and members of the D.A.R. and whose husbands were prominent in every right-wing political organization Fun City had to offer (and they have much to offer in this), were at opposite ends of the political continuum. The political activities and rhetoric of one was close to those of a liberal democrat, while the other's were nearer to those of the John Birch Society. One, while a token member of many of the same organizations, was active in politically liberal causes. The other was an active member of nearly every conservative political and social group in Fun City. Regarding her club memberships, the more liberal of the two had this to say:

. . . And, I'll tell you, I do belong to some national organizations which I have never affiliated with. I am a member of the Eastern Star and I don't want any part of it. I mean not that there is anything wrong with it, except that I don't like (and will not play) bridge although I am a good player. I won't even let 'em know I play. I hate that stuff, because it's tiresome. *And I've been a member of the Daughters of the American Revolution for 40 years and I've never gone to one single meeting anywhere. But I was sort of forced into it when I was a girl.* [Emphasis added.] I do belong to The Society of Mayflower Descendants and we have a branch (elsewhere) that I go to with one lady from here once in a while. My husband is very active in the Masonic Lodge and the church, and we're well known in town, mostly because of him. . . . They just suddenly realized he had a wife, a lot of them thought he was a bachelor [laugh] cause they didn't ever see me, you know. And he's an awful kidder. He kids and jollies 'em along and that sort of thing. I think it's a little bit overdone sometimes, but he doesn't.

The above gives some indication of the sharp behavioral and attitudinal differences that can be found within political groups (in some cases greater than those found between them). Further, contradictions can be found in voting behavior. One staunch Republican noted, on the question of Governor Reagan's performance:

Oh, I didn't vote for him but I think he's done a good job. At the time he went in I thought well, he comes from a movie background, what does he know? You know. But I've changed my mind and I think he's doing the best that anyone could. He tries. He's trying to bring in welfare reforms and a lot of other different things, but he's been blocked at every turn. . . . Then they get some of these people that are getting two or three thousand dollars a year on welfare. Well, that's as much as I've got to live on. Sometimes I think maybe I'll go on welfare.

The above is not to be taken literally. Actually my informant requires more like seven or eight thousand dollars a year to live in Fun City, and I doubt very much that she has ever really thought of going on welfare.

Another woman, a liberal Democrat, told of how (regarding her choice of Humphrey or McGovern in the presidential nomination race) she changed her mind the night before the vote and voted for Humphrey even though she felt McGovern was the better man. When asked why, she said that she felt that Humphrey had looked so bad during the TV debate the preceding evening, she felt sorry for him. "Someone had to vote for him, didn't they?" Conversations with Fun City residents were shot through with political and logical inconsistencies of this kind.

One man, a Republican, Mason, and American Legionnaire, was very much against President Nixon's political and economic policies. It was the President's policies he felt that were responsible for the current economic slump and his losses on the market. As you might expect, he was also very much against communism and socialism, and in particular the Soviet Union and the "Red Chinese." Having acknowledged all of this, he went on to say that looking at the world picture, in his opinion it was only the dictatorships that were thriving. Democracy is all right except for the fact you can't rely on the judgment of the common people. They're "fickle" and ought not to be trusted. He did not believe, as Winston Churchill did, that "Democracy was the worst possible form of government, except all the others." He favored dictatorships. One had only to look to see. "Look at the 'Red Chinese' and Russians. They're thriving."

The range of political inconsistency is difficult to imagine if one operates on a rational decision-making model of human behavior. The following clipping from the *Fun City News* gives some indication of what might serve as one end point on a "political inconsistency" continuum.

Although next year is an election year, the [Fun City's] Republican Assembly appears to be so busy socializing that they are letting "Herman do it" in registering new voters.

While [Fun City] is preponderantly Republican, and votes Republican, it would seem the leaders of that party would take enough interest to do a little registering themselves.

Instead of "letting George do it," they've let Herman, and the Herman we are referring to is Herman, president of the Democratic club, and a deputy registrar.

Herman tells us that in the last five months, he has registered at his table in the Shopping Center some 700 voters, "and most of them were Republicans."

One might reasonably expect such contradictions to lead to internal and external forms of conflict—internal, in that statements are logically inconsistent (frequently mutually exclusive even within the same sentence); external, because political discussions with one's neighbors taking the above form, seem certain to lead to controversy and confusion. Notwithstanding the reasonableness of the above assumption, it rarely happens that way. Residents seem to have little or no problems with the internal inconsistency of their statements. Neither do they argue among themselves. The latter is true primarily because of the avoidance techniques (noted earlier) of not giving offense. The following account describes its operation, with regard to Fun City politics.

Mrs. B.: But here it's [the forms of interaction] mostly . . .

Mr. B.: Social.

Mrs. B.: Social, recreational, that's what it is. And, as they say, when you reach that age . . . a lot of people miss the other kind [intellectual and political forms of interaction].

Dr. J.: Some of the things that you used to like were more intellectual and political and they don't have much [of that] here.

Mrs. B.: There is none, not much, there is none.

Dr. J.: There isn't any?

Mrs. B.: Excepting the Democratic club and it's dull as you can make it, because being poor, a Democratic club hasn't got the money to have a good speaker come out or something like that. They haven't got it. So I don't ever go to a Democratic meeting because I know exactly what it is going to be. They'll talk about the fire house. They spoke here for months and months [about the fire house]. That doesn't belong to a Democratic organization, it belongs to the association, to the Civic Association. See, but I mean, this is not the business of a Democratic club, a political Democratic club has different issues to take up. So I wasn't interested. I stopped going. Or they had a cemetery business. For months and months they talked about a cemetery [how to prepare for and keep burial costs low]. I mean what sort of a political organization [is that]? Do you understand what I mean?

Dr. J.: Yeah, there are a lot of issues but they don't seem like very significant political issues for you.

Mrs. B.: That's what it is. It's not a Democratic· club that has taken an interest [in] worldly affairs.

Mr. B.: Well, local and county politics, oh, yeah.

Mrs. B.: Anyway, why should I argue with you [with Mr. B.]. In other words, it isn't much of an interest to go. If you don't go to a meeting you don't miss much.

Dr. J.: Uh huh.

Mrs. B. That's what I mean. But one that is a hundred percent Democrat, still goes to the meetings, and when he comes home, well what happened? Nothing. Every time he [her husband] comes home, I say, well what happened at the meetings? Nothing. . . .

Mr. B.: You see, like one little activity we belong to [is] the United Nations Association. And they made me chairman of the group here in Fun City. We have about six or seven members. Out of the six, seven members [out of a total population of about six thousand] I think all but the exception of one, I brought them in to belong, and we go to Missionville [an adjacent town] to meetings once every month.

Mrs. B.: Well there is no group here [no chapter of the U.N. Association in Fun City].

Mr. B.: I'm trying to organize a chapter here. Well, a lot of people here that I approach and speak to they say now this is a communist organization, and that settles it. But I am not a, say like a professional organizer, pusher, but that's the least I can do [to try to get a chapter started].

Dr. J.: What are some of the political things going on? I mean either locally in Fun City, or nationally. Where do they stand on big issues? For example, a big thing I suppose is the war. What do people think about it?

Mr. B.: Well, you see as I said. We like to be neighborly and friendly and if I speak to someone and if his views don't coincide with mine well right away we'll change [the subject]. We'll change, we'll talk about fishing.

Dr. J.: Change the subject?

Mr. B.: We'll talk about fishing or hunting or something like that, do you see. That's the best way. And lately, you know, this business with the bombing, Nixon's bombing of the North Vietnamese.

Dr. J.: Yeah.

Mrs. B.: He's [the neighbor] a hundred percent in favor of it. Now how can you already be friendly when your political views are so different. There is a twain and we can't [get] close to one another. We overlook it.

Dr. J.: You just don't talk about politics?

Mrs. B.: That's right. When Joe [the neighbor] told me his opinion of the bombing he says, he's [President Nixon] doing the right thing, he should have done it longer [a long time ago].

Mr. B.: He is entitled to his opinion . . . a lot of people high in office or in education they are in the same opinion. [Mr. B. is not of that opinion.] See, so you can't argue politics.

Mrs. B.: In other words in order to keep the friendship that we developed and it is good for us [to be friendly] we pay no attention to his opinion. We stick to our own opinion and we give him the privilege of his own.

Dr. J.: So you don't talk about controversial things.

Mrs. B.: No, we don't clash.

Mr. B.: [Sometimes] we can get together either in their house or mine and we play a simple game [of cards] and spend a few hours and then have a cup of tea and talk. And [we] try to avoid gossip, that's the most important thing. See, but once people start gossiping then it is bad because you can't control what your'e saying, you see. [It's hard to censor yourself and you may inadvertently say something that would give offense.] And before I finished the sentence that I want to her [that he's spoken to his wife], the rest of the town knows. So you have to be on the lookout.

Mr. B.: And especially amongst the Jews, its a very small town.

Mr. B.: So in other words, I like the way she said, the small town. It is a small town but people come here from some big [towns] you know.

Dr. J.: Big towns?

Mr. B.: Big town centers, but when they come here they become small towners. And [like living in the country] they like it or something like that. In general, I think as I said before, most of the people are happy here that they retired [to Fun City].

Mrs. B.: I don't think so. It is very unnatural if you want my opinion. Personally I think it's unnatural. Because youth needs age and age needs youth. We have to have all kinds in order to have a normal community.

Mr. B.: Well didn't we have it for sixty, seventy years? That's enough.

Mrs. B.: That's all right. What makes you think that it was bad? [Having youth around.]

Mr. B.: Well, I was glad to get out of it.

Mrs. B: The old should be surrounded by youth and youth should observe age, and that would be . . .

Mr. B.: But do they respect age?

Mrs. B.: I am not talking about respect. I am talking about normal things . . . And this town is unnatural. Because there is no such thing as old, old age, and nothing but. See, it takes away normalcy. It isn't normal.

Mr. B.: But I am sorry I would disagree with you.

Mrs. B.: But that's my opinion.

Mr. B.: This is not a closed town, it's open. There are hundreds of sales people here, waitresses, service, all kinds, these lawnmowers [gardeners], and they all live around here, five or six miles away, and they spend here all the time. We see them. We see children every weekend.

Mrs. B.: Uh huh, but we see them and what happens? When we see a young child [the residents go] "Cluck, cluck, cluck." You see, as if either they are little animals unusual to us or we become the zoo to them. Now that shouldn't be. I disapprove of the whole thing.

Segments of the above account (see pp. 63–65) are characteristic not only of Fun City politics and how some of its contradictions are assimilated, but are also examples of a political split within the same household by spouses holding the same formal political affiliations. This political split extends itself to include the more general features of their current way of life. Mr. B. seems to enjoy the peace and quiet that the geographical and social isolation of Fun City has to offer. Mrs. B. considers the entire state of affairs "unnatural" and would prefer to deal with the discord that stems from being a member of the larger community.

PERVERSE DEMOCRACY

Notwithstanding the built-in conservatism of Fun City politics and the discriminatory policies it includes, there are certain "democratic" leveling influences at work. For example, there are many Fun City residents who are generally unimpressed with what others "used to be" or "used to do." This general indifference to the former status of their neighbors was, I believe, outstanding. After all, there were many formerly wealthy, powerful, and influential persons among Fun City residents. For example, President Nixon used to serve as a process-server for

Mr. S. "Nick" (the president) later took his superior's slot in the law firm when the latter moved up. Some residents are even now only semiretired and act as consultants to various firms having considerable influence, not only within Fun City but in the larger community. Still, they are not what they once were, and others, recognizing this, soon tire of hearing about their former influence, status, and position. Allowing that some formerly influential persons may find a ready audience among other formally influential persons (for example in the stock exchange room of the bank during morning "bull sessions," or at the Ladies Club) the general attitude of Fun City residents toward boasting or name-dropping ranges from boredom to resentment. This stems not only from the residents' recognition that others are not what they once were, but also from the tacit understanding that one should neither give nor take offense.

The latter influence had its origin in several sources. First was a kind of bourgeois gentility characteristic of many Fun City residents. Second was the theme of the "common enemy." This referred to the citizens in the neighboring towns, to whom Fun City residents pay substantial school taxes and for which they receive no benefits; the younger generation who neither understood nor cared for the aged and who had "peculiar" or "immoral" ways; the greater outside political process that had long ignored the economic and social needs of older persons; those responsible for the country's current economic plight; and that amorphous mass responsible for the lack of "law and order in the streets"—"coloreds," "communists," "hippies," and "welfare types," who are now found everywhere. There is, in short, the feeling that older persons in general, and Fun City residents in particular, need to stick together. Even if we recognize and allow for the social bond that stems from these influences, it is in no way sufficient to unite everyone in pursuing a common purpose. Fun City residents, as residents elsewhere, to a large extent pursue their own self-interests. However, insofar as social separation and the principle of not giving offense operate, in conjunction with the infirmities of age, the unity that stems from "consciousness of kind," and the binding effects that results from their view of "the common enemy," the self-interests of many Fun City residents have much in common. The net result is the residents' feeling that they are "as good as the next person" or at least as good as any other Fun City resident. One woman summed up part of the above process as follows:

> And I'll be honest with you, sometimes when I go to a large meeting down here at [Fun City] Town Hall, I look around and at first I used to get a feeling of repulsion. Because something about older people, they are ugly. They don't look nice. . . . But now that I've been here longer I've overlooked that and I just see my friends. I recognize faces now and people I know that are glad to see me. And suddenly I come tight with that old feeling, well, sister, who do you think you are? Perhaps you're not so hot either. After all your figure is going, your hair is getting grey, you're getting brown spots on your hands and I think, 'oh, brother this business of getting old, the aging process. But where on Earth would they [the residents of Fun City] go. This is a retreat. It's sort of a false paradise in a way. We're not of the world and yet do we want to be?

THE *FUN CITY NEWS*: A REFLECTION OF POLITICAL ATTITUDES

The *Fun City News* carries little national or international news. It reports, instead, upon local events, human interest stories, club activities, obituaries, and so on. For the most part the *News*, like most Fun City communications, keeps to the noncontroversial.

On those occasions when it takes a position on national or international events, it is invariably against labor, ecology movements, welfare, the Soviet Union, "Red China," and for management, industry, "melting pot," Vietnam war, death penalty, free enterprise, and "law and order." The following excerpts from the *Fun City News*, taken over a year's period, are illustrative:

On Industry

American business is under attack. If the attack succeeds, the business system which has produced this country's prosperity will be destroyed or seriously impaired. Unfortunately, there is no sign of a major counter-attack by free enterprise forces.

A hate-business climate is developing rapidly. Ralph Nader's continuing campaign against business has contributed substantially to this climate. The Nader reports have been published in pocketbook form and are available on book racks around the country. Mr. Nader also lectures widely and appears frequently on TV. His charges and complaints go virtually unanswered.

The corporation also is under attack on the campus. For example, this year the John Fitzgerald Kennedy School of Government at Harvard organized a study group on "Corporate Power in a Liberal Democracy."

The school's announcement said that "Corporate Power is a major public issue once again after two decades of complacent assurance that the reforms of the Progressive and New Deal periods had subjected American industry to effective public control."

The U.S. corporation represents the constructive force in the nation—the doers. Thus it is under attack from the Liberal-Left ideologues and from the talkers who speak glibly of "radically restructuring" American society.

What is the alternative to the American corporation?

The only alternative is a government agency—an enterprise controlled by bureaucrats. This isn't a valid alternative.

The history of many nations shows that government agencies are inefficient producers and managers. The move from a free enterprise system to a socialist system is a reactionary, backward step. Yet that is the direction in which the critics of the U.S corporation are attempting to move the country.

They are determined to turn back the clock to statism. But business must make that fact clear to the U.S. public.

Business must speak out and explain how the hate-the-corporation attitude is destructive of the comfortable life enjoyed by the American people.

On Unionism

What can be done [to curb "union monopoly power"]? Efforts must be stepped up to curb the unions and to make them subject to antitrust laws. The public must insist that the government stop rewarding welfare and food stamp parasites who, in effect, loot our society. Moochers must be put to work. Every working man or woman in this country must make an effort to increase productivity to offset the high wage scales. The courts must strike down union rules which forbid productivity increases.

These changes are essential if American industry is to survive and the Pittsburghs of America are to retain their economic vitality.

Another article goes:

Monopoly unionism which can paralyze the nation's economy is one of America's most serious problems. The United States won't be able to recover its economic health unless the union monopolists are curbed. . . .

It is shocking that a handful of union officials should be able to halt ocean commerce through the port of New York and other seaports, or that coal—essential to the electric power industry—should cease to be mined on the orders of union leaders.

Union bosses who issue such orders . . . are the equivalent of the robber barons of medieval times. They hold up essential commerce in our society. They cost seaport cities millions of dollars per day in lost business.

Something must be done about such modern-day highway robbery, about such an abuse of power that violates the rights of millions of working people, manufacturers and communities. And, at long last, something is being done in Congress. Last month, U.S. Rep. Sam Steiger of Arizona introduced a National Right to Work law. Thus, for the first time, a serious drive is being mounted for a national ban on compulsory unionism. Seventeen other congressmen are co-sponsors of this important legislation.

The sponsors of this legislation don't expect victory this year. But they have started a legislative process that offers great hope to a nation weakened by union tyranny.

On Environment

Repercussions from the disastrous vote on the SST [Super-Sonic Transport] in Congress last week continues to be heard from many sectors of the economy and it is my educated guess that things will get worse before they get better for those who helped deal this cruel blow to the aerospace industry—one half of which is situated in Southern California.

Top victors in the weird struggle which resulted in demise of the SST by certain politicians have been the love children on their perennial ecology crusade at the expense of American science and technology which they have linked emotionally to the "military-industrial complex."

What really won over the thinking of those who voted against the SST on Capital Hill? Most likely, not the arguments usually cited . . . but a cold calculating eye on the 18-year-old vote, the hippies, the youthful voices who have made the "ecology" their number one concern at the expense of American strength on the world stage and the domestic front at home.

On Vietnam (My Lai)

The verdict in the court martial of First Lt. William L. Calley, Jr., is causing grave concern and anguish throughout the country. Great numbers of thoughtful citizens fear that the verdict will seriously damage morale and combat effectiveness in the U.S. armed forces. . . . The criticism should be directed elsewhere. It should be directed at the peacenik bloc in the Senate, at the merchants of defeatism who monopolize reporting of the news on television, at the academic advocates of surrender to communism, and at the architects of "no-win" strategy in Vietnam—former President Lyndon Johnson and former Secretary of Defense Robert S. McNamara. . . .

In assessing the verdict in the Calley trial, Americans should bear in mind that the events at My Lai were used by the enemies of the United States in a world-wide effort to discredit the United States. Moscow and Hanoi must have been vastly pleased when the U.S. Army was pressured into ordering court martial proceedings against American officers and enlisted men. The Communists succeeded in having the U.S. Army placed on trial. . . .

The Fulbrights and the McGoverns are the leaders who should be on trial in the court of public opinion. If any element has bloody hands as a result of the Vietnam War, it is the hypocritical "peace" group in the senate—the appeaser Senators who opposed bombing and blockading of North Vietnam. Had the military professionals been allowed to undertake these measures, there would have been no need for a long, bitter, bloody conflict in the isolated hamlets of Southeast Asia.

On Hippies

One of the distinctive features of the 1970's is an inward-turning attitude on the part of many Americans.

On the lunatic fringe there is the phenomenon of the urban or rural commune where young people experiment in group living without formalities or responsibilities. Strange new cults flourish in some of our major cities. The Manson trial in California lifted the lid on weird beliefs and practices in the midst of our modern society. . . .

Perhaps the hippie style of life is the ultimate luxury in an affluent society. In societies where a stern struggle for life is the rule, the hippie is unknown. Dressing in beads, Indian head bands and fringed leather clothes can be regarded as a form of conspicuous consumption.

Whatever the psychological motivation—and the clothes indicate an inner dissatisfaction with reality, the United States can ill afford continuing indulgence in the hippie outlook—the inward-looking attitude in any form. . . .

Working citizens can't be expected to carry the hippie elements on their back for years on end. There's no moral obligation on good citizens to subsidize or protect these people who won't accept any of the burdens or responsibilities of a person living in society.

In the last few years our country has gone on a binge of toleration insofar as irresponsible people are concerned. It is time to insist on a new measure of social discipline and respect for public authority.

It is time to demand that those who want to look inward and avoid the realities be brought face to face with the requirements of citizenship. The "hip" cultists can't be permitted to disrupt and spoil our society.

On Censorship and Pornography

The case for censorship of the pornography now sweeping across America in a filthy tide has been ably stated by Irving Kristol, editor of *The Public Interest* journal and professor of urban values at New York University.

In a recent essay published in the *Chicago Tribune*, Prof. Kristol asserts—and rightly so—that "if you care for the quality of life in our American democracy, then you have to be for censorship."

This is a point of view currently unfashionable in liberal circles, and Prof. Kristol is to be commended for taking a principled stand.

In explaining his position, Prof. Kristol points out that in the United States censorship "has to all intents and purposes ceased to exist."

The federal courts have lowered virtually all the legal barriers to the distribution and showing of pornographic material.

Civil libertarians of the past, he says, wanted freedom for serious literary works that were not wholly in keeping with public standards. "They have got that, of course," he notes, "but they have also got a world in which homosexual rape takes place on the stage, in which the public flocks during lunch hours to witness varieties of professional fornication, in which Time Square in New York City has become little more than a hideous market for the sale and distribution of printed filth that panders to all known perversions."

It is this condition that makes clear the need for censorship in some form. . . .

A nation has to be concerned about the quality of its citizenry. It has to legislate against elements and developments which brutalize and debase its people. In a self-governing society, it is necessary to care about the character of the people, and guard against the spread of degeneracy.

Society has the right to draw a line on human behavior and on self-expression. It has a right to forbid physical torture on a stage, Prof. Kristol comments, "even if the victim were a willing masochist." By definition, society involves rules and value-judgments.

In the past, U.S. authorities made the necessary judgments regarding pornography and devised rules to control the traffic.

The U.S. Supreme Court, in a series of decisions, gave the pornographers—the smut-peddlers—a green light.

The need now is to build a new American consensus on the subject of printed and filmed filth, emphasizing the importance of strengthening the quality of our national life. This new consensus should produce corrective decisions by the courts.

All thoughtful, decent Americans should be able to agree on the legislative action to prevent the distribution of material that debases human relationships.

On Prison Reforms

A policeman riddled with bullets from the gun of an ex-con gives the average man on the street cause to think about the rehabilitation systems offered in California prisons.

Convicted felons are boosted back on the streets as fast as parole and probation authorities can move them. . . .

Convictions for felonies have nearly doubled but the prison population remains the same. Does this mean that we are as safe on the streets today as we were in 1961? . . .

Since 1966, when sociologists convinced the state legislature to approve the "probation subsidy" program, California has operated generally on the principle that the convicted felon stands a better chance of rehabilitation if he is not removed from his county and family by being sent to a state prison.

With the rapid increase in crimes by former convicted felons, some lawmakers are beginning to wonder if this lenient treatment is justified. Perhaps the convicted felon would stand a better chance at rehabilitation if he did "hard time" in a state prison. . . .

These facts led Howard W. Chappel, chairman of Los Angeles Mayor Sam Yorty's narcotics commission, to say:

It is not in the best interest of our national security to continually plan on the rehabilitation of future generations because certain segments of our population, for whatever reason, do not want to quarantine drug peddlers for extended periods of time.

California's system of rehabilitation, probation and parole appears to be in trouble.

CONCLUSION

While it is true that in terms of political attitudes Fun City is not very different from other communities within a fifty-mile radius of it or Middle American towns in general, it is atypical in many other regards. We have already noted its geographical isolation, the absence of a police department, fire department, major medical facilities, the fact that all residents are over 50 years of age, that there is no industry and few jobs, an average "fixed income" of $8,000 per year, and that both the appearance of the community and the nature of interaction within it can only be described as gray on gray. Then too, since the majority of Fun City residents were recruited from a nearby metropolitan area as opposed to the smaller adjacent communities, many, upon retiring to Fun City, experienced a "culture shock." The early inhabitants were especially vocal in noting how they had moved from a comfortable residential middle-class environment to a "dust bowl" or a "duck swamp." While those who settled in Fun City some years later had more of the amenities they were formerly accustomed to, such as streets and sidewalks, the fact remains that the gestalt, Fun City, was very different from the environment most residents had spent their lives in. Residents readily volunteered that it took "a lot of getting used to." We have dealt throughout with the ways in which those who remained in Fun City attempted to adapt. In particular, an effort was made to describe these modes of adaptation in terms of the residents' day-to-day existence.

5 / Some theories of aging:
A test of goodness of fit

In this concluding chapter, we will consider some of the more popular concerns and theoretical positions toward aging in general and retirement in particular, and the extent to which the explicit and implicit expectations generated by these theories fit the life styles of Fun City residents. I will begin by considering the various ways in which the aged are usually studied. In an essay entitled "Principles of Research on Aging" Birren (1959:16–17) lists four basic types of studies:

1. Studies of longevity constitute one of the more clearly recognized types in which length of life is regarded as dependent on a variety of independent variables such as genetic background, parental age. . . . In human longevity, inferences about the influences of the independent variables are almost exclusively limited to those derived from statistical analysis, where animal studies allow for direct manipulation of selected variables.
2. Another type of study is concerned with differences with age in a broad range of biological, psychological, and social characteristics. . . . Chronological age is used initially as the independent variable, but, as this type of investigation progresses, the resulting explanations do not usually include age or time.
3. A third general type of study is concerned with problems of how a complex living organism moves forward in time. . . . The biological and behavioral chronology of the individual involves phases or stages of development and aging, such as pubescence and menopause, which have a distinct constellation of characteristics.
4. A fourth type of study is concerned with the historical aspects of the experience of an individual or group. . . . This type of study includes identification of those aspects of the individual's biology and psychology which remain stable or characteristic of him in comparison with the group. Interest lies in identifying these aspects or patterns of the individual which will remain distinctive of him over the life span.

Conspicuously absent from these four basic approaches to gerontological research is unobtrusive participant-observer studies, or ethnographic studies of the aged in natural settings. Birren's essay first appeared in 1959, but things have not changed appreciably since then. The four types of studies outlined are still representative of those found in the literature. There are very few exceptions. In an article five years later (Rose 1964) and in my introduction to this work it is noted that the need for empirical studies of the aged is as strong as the existing literature is weak. Participant-observer studies of the life styles of the aged, in conjunction

72

with interviews of the aged in various social settings over time, are conspicuously absent. Without such descriptive material we cannot proceed scientifically—that is, describe and classify phenomena by their common characteristics so as to be able to link them conceptually into a consistent and parsimonious system of explanation that will provide for understanding, prediction, and control. The absence of theory (defined in this way) from the existing gerontological literature is, therefore, not surprising.

There are, however, numerous interesting and insightful notions about aging that can be profitably considered and compared to the findings in Fun City. For example, an interesting general formulation of adult socialization, with implications for explaining personal change in the life style of the aged, is Becker's (1964) article entitled "Personal Change in Adult Life." It provides a conceptual framework which can be used to explain the consistency found among Fun City residents in terms of their strong commitment to conflict avoidance, quite apart from the various temperaments or personalities involved. A key feature of this process is Becker's notion of situational adjustment (1964:44):

> One of the most common mechanisms in the development of the person in adulthood is the process of situational adjustment. . . . The person as he moves in and out of a variety of social situations, learns the requirements of continuing in each situation and of success in it. If he has a strong desire to continue, the ability to assess accurately what is required, and can deliver the required performance, the individual turns himself into the kind of person the situation demands.

Such a frame of reference, as it applies to the Fun City resident, would mean that if one were committed to remaining in Fun City, he would have to assess what was required of him (the key requirement of not giving offense is unambiguously given from the outset) and, no matter how congenial or offensive this requirement seemed, abide by it at all cost. "Keep the peace" is the watchword. The question of whether or not this peace results in a social setting worth retaining is a problem studiously avoided by the residents. To the extent that Fun City residents are reluctant or unable to move (for reasons outlined earlier), many have a commitment to staying. Those who remain come from different religious, political, and occupational backgrounds, notwithstanding the fact that most residents share a similar socioeconomic status. In spite of the differences between active and inactive persons, high-key–low-key types, different temperaments, personalities, and interests of residents, all seemed to conform to the major behavioral expectation of "not giving offense" and "getting along." We have already considered the various devices invoked to accomplish this end and the relative success (and expense) of this general undertaking. The entire procedure can be seen to occur within the general process of situational adjustment. The notion of situational adjustment is, in my opinion, applicable as well to earlier stages of the life cycle and need not be restricted to changes in adult life.

Another interesting position on aging is found in an essay by Gordon F. Streib (1965), entitled "Are the Aged a Minority Group?" Streib concludes that they are not. He notes that those sociologists who believe the aged do comprise a minority group "rarely test their assumptions by referring to all of the elements of Wirth's definition." Wirth defines (Streib 1965:312) a minority group as follows:

> . . . people who, because of physical or cultural characteristics are singled out from the others in the society in which they live for differential and unequal treatment, and who therefore regard themselves as objects of collective discrimination. The existence of a minority in a society implies the existence of a corresponding dominant group with higher social status and greater privileges. Minority status carries with it the exclusion from full participation in the life of society.

Having reformulated this definition into six major points, Streib sets about showing that since the aged are not subject to the above constraints they do not comprise a minority group. A large part of his refutation rests upon considering the aged as individuals who are not yet retired or if retired are not in an isolated, planned, homogeneous retirement setting. A growing number of the aged, defined as persons over sixty or over sixty-five, are retired. Among those, more and more are retiring to retirement communities that have much in common with Fun City. This being the case, much of Streib's refutation of the aged as a minority group, as it relates to retired persons in planned retirement settings, is inapplicable. For example, the aged in the retirement settings do exhibit many of the features associated with minority group status that Streib feels are absent among the aged who are still working and a part of the greater community.

Fun City residents exhibit "a sense of consciousness of kind," are subject to "restrictions on political roles and activities," do not have "access to work," are "subject to residential segregation" (by way of subjecting others to it), do experience "social [and geographic] isolation," are as a group looked upon by the greater community as "less deserving of respect and consideration" (indeed, this is their self-perception of how others view them), and experience "less economic and social security" (real or perceived): It is true, of course, that many of the other features Streib has outlined as characteristic of minority groups do not apply to Fun City residents—for example, they do not "possess identifying characteristics with accompanying status-role expectations throughout the life cycle" nor are their civil rights sometimes denied.

However, as more of the aged retire to retirement settings of the type of Fun City, Streib's six-point outline applies to a greater number of the aged, who are more and more taking on the features of a minority group. If we accept Wirth's definition as is, then there is an even better fit between the definition of a minority group and the life style of Fun City residents. For example, Fun City residents, because of their physical characteristics (old age and illness) are singled out from others in society as a whole for differential and unequal treatment, and do consider themselves objects of collective discrimination by those comprising this society, while they are certainly excluded (by choice or otherwise) from full participation.

In short, the numerous studies that Streib cites to help support his argument that the aged do not comprise a minority group are studies of the aged, but not studies of the retired aged, nor of retired persons in planned, isolated, homogeneous retirement settings. Insofar as the trend is toward earlier retirement and retirement in the above form of retirement setting, Streib's argument no longer has the strength it may have once had. Indeed, I must agree with Rose (1962:127), who feels the aged are taking on more of the features of a minority group all the time.

> There is a desire to associate with fellow-agers, especially in formal associations, and to exclude the younger adults from these associations. These are expressions of group pride and corollary expressions of dismay concerning the evidence of deterioration in the outgroup—the younger generation. . . . These are manifestations of a sense of resentment at "the way elderly people are being mistreated" and of taking social action to remove the source of their resentment. These are the signs of group identification that previous sociological studies have found in ethnic minority groups. . . . I do not mean to exaggerate this parallel, nor to state that most older people today show most of these signs, but the evidence of growing group identification among older people in the United States today is available to even the casual observer.

In the article quoted, "The Subculture of Aging," Rose (1962:125) "looks forward to empirical testing" but notes that:

> There are many other areas of the aging subculture [apart from status] that could be analyzed and speculated about. Their self-conceptions, their attitudes toward death, marriage, their interpersonal relationships and leisure [etc.] . . . There is perhaps less basis for speculation about these topics, in the almost complete absence of empirical data. . . .

This study of Fun City represents one of the few efforts to narrow this gap in the literature. The following are some implications of the author's work as they relate to Rose's position.

Much of what Rose contends regarding status is borne out by my own findings. For example, Rose's hypothesis regarding the carry-over of prestige (1962:124) among the aged in general was true of Fun City residents as well.

> As previous holding of power and earlier achievements fade into the past, they are of diminishing influence in conferring prestige. . . . If they [the aged] have changed communities, occupational prestige after retirement must go down markedly, and the other factors must be of reduced importance. If the aged individual is socially isolated, as sometimes happens, these factors in former status carry current prestige only as a sort of legend.

We have noted the operation of this factor in the preceding chapter under the discussion of "Perverse Democracy." Also borne out was his hypothesis (Rose, 1962:124) that:

> . . . older people may be more involved in a general culture than are middle-aged persons; this is in that older people lose some of the other subcultural variations—based upon class, religion, sex and possibly even ethnic identification—characteristics of the middle-age population. . . .

I also believe Rose's formulation of the untoward effects of forced retirement at age 65 is valid. This practice has led to defining the aged more narrowly, which in turn may help lead to a group identity and perhaps to political action on behalf of the group, but I feel that its negative consequences outweigh any possible benefits to be derived. The group identity that may result will, I feel, have more negative effects than are now anticipated. For example, while group identity can be viewed as positive with respect to organizing a set of persons toward purposeful actions, an identity based upon the virtues of old age and that is achieved by "putting down" youth and segregating the aged from youth in retirement settings such as Fun City, will not lead to the fulfillment of group goals through the group's greater involvement with the general culture. Nor is the general culture likely to benefit from such an identity formation and from the group's withdrawal. Some indication of the contribution that can be made by those over 65 and of the loss that would result from their withdrawal is given in an article in the New York *Times* (September 22, 1972:39):

> The State Commissioner of Human Rights announced today that a survey of more than 100,000 State employees has shown that workers over the age of 65 performed their jobs "about equal to and sometimes noticeably better than younger workers." The survey, undertaken in 40 state agencies at the request of Governor Rockefeller, was designed to support a move by the Governor to remove all age restrictions from the employment-discrimination provision of the state's human-rights laws. . . . The State survey . . . covered the areas of absenteeism due to illness, accidents or unexplained reasons, punctuality in reporting to work, on-the-job accidents, disabling or otherwise, and over-all work performance.

In an insightful article dealing with the problem of retirement within a work-leisure perspective, Stephen J. Miller (1965:80) offers an outline of three major work–leisure traditions:

> (1) pre-industrial: traditional work alleviated by related practices, and rites; (2) industrial: the polar opposition of work and leisure, and (3) post-industrial, or contemporary: the integration of work and leisure.

The problem of retired persons in integrating work and leisure in the *current* work–leisure tradition revolves around the fact that the latter is only justified in terms of the former. The dilemma is outlined as follows:

> . . . the work which a person is ultimately free of (in retirement) is exactly that which allows him to justify leisure or, as Mead has put it, work is not only necessary to obtain the means *but the right to leisure.* (Miller 1965:83) [Emhpasis added.]

This results in the retirement age person having to meet certain conditions in order to successfully establish a new and acceptable identity.

> The older person, in order to establish a new identity and acceptable self-concept on the basis of leisure must first establish a rationale for the activity on which he bases that new or altered identity. He must legitimatize it in some manner other than in those terms which sanction leisure for the very young and old. The leisure activity of the retired and elderly must, therefore, be in some way appropriate in terms of traditional and contemporary values which do not apply specifically to the aging but to the population in general. (Miller 1965:84)

This in turn may be accomplished as follows:

> He [the retired person] may do so by introducing, in much the same fashion as leisure has been introduced into work, aspects of work into his leisure. (Miller 1965:84–85)

Miller goes on to note that:

> The problems posed by aging and retirement have been well documented, but the manner in which the aging introduce aspects of work into leisure and establish an appropriate rational for this has, to the writers knowledge, been explored only incidentally. (1965:85)

The current study has a direct bearing on this problem. Miller's formulation has a very good "fit" with the way in which many Fun City residents try to make their leisure time meaningful and acceptable in terms of their prior "work ethic." Numerous examples were cited in Chapter 3 under "The Role of Employment" or within the discussion of the range of activity or inactivity of Fun City residents. For example, the Fun City Drama Club put on performances for the older and more infirm residents of the adjacent nursing home; wood shop members built the enclosures that housed emergency oxygen tanks distributed about Fun city activity centers; one resident transcribed books into braille for the blind, church volunteer groups put on clothes drives for the needy in adjacent Jonesville, others served as volunteers in a near-by hospital, and the art and ceramic clubs contributed completed projects for display in Fun City buildings as well as elsewhere. All these activities can be viewed as attempts by the residents to make their leisure-time activities meaningful and legitimate, that is, to introduce aspects of work into their leisure-time pursuits in much the same way as leisure was formerly introduced into the routine of work. The current study not only tends to support Miller's position regarding the aged's need to legitimize their leisure activities, but also shows in a formal sense the ways in which they undertake to do so.

Perhaps the most controversial contribution to gerontological theory is Cumming and Henry's (1961) notion of "disengagement." That the concept of disengagement has stimulated so much controversy and research attests to the paucity of theory in the literature. The validity and general applicability of the disengagement theory has come under serious attack from many quarters. Two good critiques can be found in the works of Arnold M. Rose (1964:89) and Raymond G. Kuhlen (1968:115–136).

Rose (1964), in an essay entitled "A Current Theoretical Issue in Social Gerontology," takes Cumming and Henry to task on a number of points. Rose notes that research in social gerontology usually takes one of two basic orientations: it is "explicitly or implicitly guided by interactionist theory, broadly conceived" or "has tended to be descriptive or interpret the facts of aging in an historical cultural context." One major exception is the work of Cumming, which takes "the framework of functionalist theory." The critique that follows is as much a critique of functionalism as it is of disengagement theory. Rose begins by defining disengagement by what it is not.

> It is *not* an hypothesis which states that, as people get older, they are gradually separated from their associations and their social functions. . . . Nor does the theory of disengagement state that, as people become physically feebler or chronically ill, they are thereby forced to abandon their associations and social functions. . . . Finally, the theory of disengagement does *not* say that because older people tend to have reduced income in our society, they can no longer afford to

participate in many things. . . . [The] theory of disengagement is that the society and the individual prepare *in advance* for the ultimate "disengagement" of incurable, incapacitating disease and death by an *inevitable, gradual and mutually satisfying process of disengagement from society.* (pp. 46–47) [Emphasis added.]

In accordance with functionalist thought, the individual and society, because of the inevitability of death, seek to maintain themselves in equilibrium by avoiding disruptions. With this in mind the older person prepares himself sociologically and psychologically for death by divesting himself of life's functions and associations. In this way death is not seen as a disruptive event in the life cycle of an individual or in the otherwise tranquil functioning of society. The equilibrium between man and society is maintained. This model of the aging process, and of the implicit and explicit modes of adaptation invoked by the individual and society within his framework, are subject to certain conceptual and empirical flaws. For example, Cumming herself notes that the original study "did not take into account such non-model cases as widowhood before the marriage of the last child or of work protracted past the modal age of retirement." She also recognizes individual differences in character and biological temperament. In fact, lively older persons even temporarily *increase* their recreational activities.

Another line of attack by Rose questions whether disengagement is desirable for older people and presents evidence to the contrary. A third point that Rose pursues in some detail,

> . . . acknowledges that a large proportion of the older people in the United States tend to lose many of their adult roles. But it considers this fact to be a function of American culture in this phase of its organization, not a universal for all time. . . . Many other societies accord special prestige and power to the elderly, do not disengage them from adult roles, or create new age-graded roles of importance for them. (p. 48)

In a four-point outline Rose notes what he believes are trends in American culture that may reverse the current practice in this country of disengaging older persons.

1. Modern medical science and health are allowing an ever-increasing proportion of those reaching 65 to remain in good health and physical vigor. It is doubtful (as a result of this) that vigorous people will be as content to disengage. . . .
2. Social security legislation and private pension plans and annuities are slowly increasing the economic security of the retired. If older people have more money to spare . . . they may . . . be more able and willing to continue their costlier participations.
3. . . . older people in the United States are beginning to form a social movement [take on the features of a minority group] to raise their status and privileges . . . Such a trend will influence the participation of the elderly in several ways: (a) It will provide a new engagement especially for older people: (b) It will inform the younger generations of the plight of the elderly . . . (c) It may raise the prestige and dignity of age . . .
4. The trend toward earlier retirement from chief life role . . . while now a factor causing disengagement, may eventually become an influence for re-engagement. . . . studies . . . show that the average young woman today is having her *last* child at age 26, which means that her last child is ceasing to be

dependent on her at the age of 40 to 45. Most women at this age are just not going to be willing to disengage, even though they have lost their chief life role, and are going to have strong motivations to re-engage. The same will be true of men if the age of retirement creeps downward, as some economists tell us it will. (pp. 48–49)

As I have mentioned earlier, the above is not only a critique of disengagement theory, but of functionalist theory in general. I believe the points in Rose's critique are well taken. While I am of a different branch of the interactionist school than Rose, I would certainly agree with his general proposition that cultural values and meanings are the most important elements in these interactions (between the aging themselves and between the aging and others in the society) and these are never assumed to be universal or unchanging.

Another less speculative critique of the disengagement theory is given by Kuhlen (1968:123–125) who makes the following points:

1. The index of life satisfaction (in one study) was correlated more highly with participation in older years than in middle age.

2. Dean cited a decline of "instrumentality" in the aged as support for disengagement, but Kuhlen interprets the same data as support for engagement, "The basic data in the study involved responses to questions 'What are the best things about being the age you are now?' and 'What are the worst things about being the age you are now?'" Kuhlen focuses on two of the categories into which these responses were classified: "output" and "frustrated output": "Output responses emphasized active engagement in the social environment, with focus on achievement, responsibility, power, and influence, utility, knowledge and experience. Frustrated output is the obverse of the above." Much of what Dean takes to be data indicative of "frustrated output" and supportive of disengagement in old age, Kuhlen convincingly reinterprets as falling within the "output" category and supportive of the engagement position.

3. Cumming and Henry note that: "It is a common belief that religious piety and practice increase with age. . . . On the other hand, disengagement theory would predict a decrease in the interest in religion as normative control is lessened." Kuhlen notes several studies indicating that there is in fact an increasing interest in immortality and involvement with religion among the aged.

4. Disengagement theory would predict not only that older people disengage but that they are happy to do so. Using anxiety as an indication of "maladjustment," which in turn is taken to be an indicator of unhappiness, Kuhlen lists a series of studies to show that there is increasing anxiety beyond middle age, accompanied by decreasing happiness and presumably increasing unhappiness.

Where do Fun City residents fall on the engagement–disengagement continuum? It is clear that the theory of disengagement does not have an *inevitable* or *universal* application to Fun City residents. Although there is good grounds for some of the following estimates of its applicability, other estimates are guesses. Let us begin by considering the five or six hundred active club members (about 10 percent of Fun City's population). These residents were clearly engaged. In fact, engagement in the pre- and postretirement period characterized the life style of this group. They constitute a clear counter-instance to disengagement as a general phenomenon.

Another group of residents also runs contrary to the expectations of disengagement theory. While these may be generally characterized as currently disengaged, and happy to be so, it is not something they accomplished or tended toward in old age. Disengagement was for them as much as a pre- as a postretirement way of life. How many residents comprise this category I do not know. Judging from informants' self-evaluation of their life styles and their assessment of their neighbors' life styles in the pre- and postretirement stages, I believe a conservative guess would be that 10–15 percent of all Fun City residents are now and have previously been disengaged as a way of life. This would bring to 20–25 percent those who do not fit the disengagement model.

However, there is yet another group of residents who were happily engaged in the pre- and early postretirement periods but because of a recent deterioration in their health, or in their spouses' health, have had to "drop out." Those who have suffered a forced disengagement of this kind do not fit the expectations of the disengagement model either, in that it assumes that members choose to disengage. While the above persons disengaged, it was not an undertaking that was anticipated, intentional, gradual, or welcome. I believe a substantial number of persons fit this category of Fun City residents, perhaps 25 percent.

This leaves what is probably the largest single category of residents, those who do seem to fit the disengagement model. I doubt that these exceed half of Fun City's total population. This group came to Fun City to retire. By this they mean to withdraw for the most part from the society of others, watch television, read, play an occasional game of cards, and walk the dog. While the residents comprising this group consider these activities (or lack of them) to be "taking it easy," something they look forward to doing, others—active Fun City residents and "outsiders"—refer to it as "vegetating." The latter look upon the former with a combination of pity and disdain which in turn may be seen as stemming from a set of expectations inherent in two basic ideologies. One can be found in Weber's formulation of "the protestant ethic" 'that contends *"Arbeit macht das Leben süss"* ("work makes life sweet"), and the other is the Marxian contention that man's "species nature" is free creative activity, and that those who do not (or cannot) pursue this as an end, become alienated from their own humanity. I don't mean to imply that Fun City residents are students of Weber or Marx, but rather that these frameworks can be superimposed upon the residents' activities and that the ideological positions would not be far from the attitudes of the more active residents toward the "disengagers."

In brief, judging from the activity and inactivity of Fun City residents in the pre- and postretirement periods, the process of disengagement, as that term is employed in disengagement theory, is not inevitable, universal, nor unchanging. The question of how many residents comprise the above categories and fit the disengagement model, and why, can be meaningfully accounted for only within an interactionist perspective, which considers behavioral outcomes to be situational and problematic. To consider disengagement in old age as a functional "given" and an inevitable form spontaneously established to ensure the well-being of society and its equilibrium, is an unpardonable gloss upon what even the casual observer can empirically observe in the real world.

Finally, it is clear that even for the 50 percent of Fun City residents who seem to be "disengaged," there is no proof whatever that their disengagement is either inevitable or beneficial, either for them or society. In short, that a segment of Fun City residents is found to be disengaged and enjoying it, does not per se provide proof for the validity of the disengagement theory. Indeed, a basic critique of functionalist theory is that it is unreasonable to formulate such propositions as Cumming and Henry make. In order to be able to state whether something is inevitable, universal, disposing the system to equilibrium, or "functional," one would need to know the very thing one is trying to find out: how the sum of the parts are interrelated and their mutual effects upon the whole. That is, it would assume *an understanding of how society works and why*, that given the current state of the social sciences, seems to me to be millennia away.

CONCLUSIONS

In light of this and other studies, certain broad questions present themselves for serious consideration. First, what would a "desirable" retirement community look like? Second, if we were to reverse the trend toward more segregated and isolated retirement settings, how could existing American communities be restructured to better incorporate a growing population of older persons? And finally, what are some of the special characteristics of American society that make retirement communities and the segregation of the aged likely?

There is no easy answer to these questions. However, studies such as this, conducted in a variety of existing retirement settings, promise to provide the kinds of information necessary for making intelligent guesses. If we learn enough about the nature of social interaction by first ascertaining the social meanings of social actions to the participants in a variety of social settings, then we may be able to structure social situations so that they result in preferred outcomes with respect to the predilections of the actors. In this sense, I believe that we can talk about what a desirable retirement community would look like. Unfortunately, very little information of this kind exists. While *the* answer must, in the final analysis, "await future research," any attempt to answer the first question will almost certainly have to incorporate the following set of considerations.

To begin with, it is unlikely that there can be *one* "desirable" form of retirement setting that would suit even a well-screened homogeneous population of persons. Fun City and many other such settings are attempts in this direction. There were within Fun City persons from a wide range of backgrounds, temperaments, and dispositions. While it is true that for some their initial impressions of Fun City changed for the worse over time, that is, they were disenchanted and moved to other settings (or wished that they could), others were quite content with the sedentary, uneventful, low-stress environment Fun City offered. Indeed, it was in many ways similar to their prior life style and level of expectation. On the other hand, some more active residents found Fun City to offer "never a dull moment."

In this regard it lived up to their expectations, and they, too, were reasonably content. Others, who found Fun City an "unnatural" social setting and were overtly unhappy, were defined by neighbors as "malcontents."

In short, there was within Fun City, as within any imaginable voluntary association, no matter how homogeneous, considerable diversity in likes and dislikes regarding the setting, the ability to adapt to it, the willingness to adapt, or the need to adapt. Fun City was no exception in this regard. It is in this sense that no *one* retirement setting, where fairly large numbers of persons are involved, is likely to provide a preferred setting even when the population is screened for age, race, and income as Fun City residents were.

A better arrangement would be a setting that could satisfy, albeit imperfectly, the needs of a wide range of individuals having different temperaments, former life styles, social and ethnic backgrounds, and physical capacities. This need is evident even in communities such as Fun City, but unfortunately Fun City did not have the requisite flexibility. Indeed, every effort had been made to eliminate accommodating mechanisms, with the tacit assumption—or at least hope—that such flexibility would be unnecessary. This was based on the assumptions that only white, gentile, middle-class homeowners would be encouraged to come and stay in Fun City and that this was a preferred and legitimate arrangement, in that everyone sought peace, quiet, security, gentility, and their "own kind" in their declining years. However, in an attempt to establish what one resident astutely referred to as a "false paradise," they inadvertently ensured social isolation, the establishment and maintenance of "the blasé attitude," and what many knew, but with some ambivalence accepted, as an "unnatural environment." In short, while most residents felt that they had achieved the peace and quiet they had sought, it was at a price that was higher than some had intended to pay, and higher than many others knew. For a small segment of other residents it was also more peace and quiet than they had bargained for.

In fact the structural flexibility necessary to accommodate a wide range of individual needs, which are an inherent part of relatively large groups of persons, was impossible in an isolated, segregated "homogeneous" retirement setting such as Fun City. In this regard the question of cost analysis arises. Planners and potential buyers are misguided to suppose that by screening out undesirables (potential trouble makers), moving to isolated settings to get away from trouble and trouble makers, or weeding out "undesirable elements" who have infiltrated, they can reconstruct an Eden to suit every taste. Even when they seem to succeed, as in the case of Fun City, it is not without hidden costs to the individual and the environment. Some of these have been outlined above. Any future attempt at planning retirement settings would do well to anticipate some of these hidden costs before attempting to concoct in the "melting pot" (even a very selective pot) the essence of white middle-class peace and quiet, or some other gourmet dish cooked to the dictates of a select palate. The fact is that no matter how seductive such a diet may seem, man lives better in the long run on slumgullion.

The nation has, of late, become painfully aware that the "melting pot" as an ideological ploy for dispelling differences and potential conflict and establishing "equilibrium"—peace and quiet—has failed. This is not surprising, in that catchwords have never disposed of the differences that exist between individuals and groups regarding their cultural backgrounds, work experiences, life styles, expectations, or predispositions. These are things that exist between men in groups, even homogeneous retirement groups, and it would be better to recognize and attempt to deal with these differences, than to try—futilely—to screen them out. The irony in such an undertaking lies in the fact that not only is one destined to fail but that one would be utterly undone if he succeeded. Fun City must be viewed as having been relatively successful in its screening operation, yet it must also be viewed as a relative failure as a retirement setting. This is true notwithstanding the fact that different segments of the population are reasonably content with Fun City. For most it has proved to be a "false Paradise." I believe that this is true of segregated retirement settings in general. One has, after all, grown up in "natural settings," conflictual, stressful settings that emanate from the diversity of persons, opinions, and behaviors that one encounters in the world at large. That one should wish to withdraw from this stress and confusion when one is increasingly unable to cope and best able, economically and socially, to withdraw gracefully is not surprising. However, most of us have, since the Fall, been obliged to accommodate to the imperfect state of man and go through life working for, with, and against one another. Those searching for paradise (on earth or elsewhere) seem to be uninformed by the fact that should they encounter it, they will encounter with it "culture shock" and experience it as an alien thing. It was this that made Fun City seem "unnatural." Heaven no less than Hell "will take some getting used to." Indeed, given our place of origin, we may find it more easy to accommodate to the latter.

If segregated and isolated homogeneous retirement settings are not the answer for the growing population of older persons in the United States, what are? The leads us to a consideration of the second question . . . "If we were to reverse the trend toward more segregated and isolated retirement settings, how could existing American communities be restructured to better incorporate a growing population of older persons?"

I believe the greatest promise lies in reversing this trend. An effort should be made to retain retirement settings in "natural," that is, familiar, environments. With some 70 percent of the total U.S. population living within urban-metropolitan areas, some effort should be made to integrate retirement communities into existing urban settings. While urban-based settings are unlikely to provide as much peace and tranquillity as Fun City, they also promise to provide far less isolation and alienation. The latter stems from Fun City's geographical isolation and its self-imposed social isolation. This results from the superhuman effort on the part of residents to reduce conflict to zero through segregation by age, race, and income and the mechanisms of not giving offense. Every effort is made to make Fun City peaceful and friendly.

Integrating retirement settings with existing natural settings would, if properly undertaken, ensure against geographical isolation and social isolation stemming from segregation by age, race, or class. It would also recognize that a degree of conflict is unavoidable, not necessarily disruptive, and even when disruptive, not necessarily bad. Residents would then feel free (or at least more free) to voice their opinions on a wide range of meaningful and potential controversial subjects and exhibit behaviors appropriate to the intensity of their feelings. In short, they would, depending upon their predilections and the circumstances, be able to act for, with, and against one another as they were previously accustomed to doing, within the natural constraints of everyday life. I believe such a life style would make for a more meaningful, if less placid, existence and overcome some of the more serious problems of isolated, segregated, homogeneous planned retirement settings.

How best to accomplish this integration of retirement settings into existing urban areas, in order to achieve the goals we have described, will need to await further research. Placing the setting into an urban area familiar to the resident will not of itself overcome the isolation and inactivity that is rampant in Fun City. Indeed, the author is now conducting a study of an urban-centered retirement setting that seems to exhibit many (but by no means all) of Fun City's more negative aspects. Placing retired persons into a community setting within an urban environment holds the *promise* for many of overcoming the shortcomings associated with isolated "unnatural" retirement settings. However, the question of how to best achieve these goals is something that has only recently received serious attention.

Finally, there is the question of the special characteristics of American society that are responsible for the proliferation of retirement settings. I will outline what I believe are some of the more salient features of this recent expansion. Some of these have already been considered earlier in the chapter in our discussion of theoretical contributions to the gerontological literature. For example, we have already mentioned forced retirement at age 65, financial security through increased social security benefits, pensions, and other retirement plans, the expanding mobility of the American public which allows them to entertain the prospect of retiring in unfamiliar geographical settings, longer life spans, the disintegration of the extended family, earlier retirements, expanding land developments with an eye to fast profits, development of leisure time pursuits and vacation settings, and so on. All of these have become, or are fast becoming, a part of "the American way of life." While many of them constitute the *pull* necessary for the expansion of isolated retirement settings, the *push* from the cities to unfamiliar and isolated rural-area retirement settings is being supplied by the real or imagined "crime in the streets," environmental pollution, urban congestion, and, more generally, by the difficulty one associates with coping in an urban environment.

These and other push-pull factors have come together to initiate a strong trend toward the expansion of special retirement communities. While such settings have immediate appeal, many residents soon become disenchanted with what they initially felt was an ideal setting. Some of the reasons for this disenchantment, regarding Fun City in particular and isolated segregated retirement settings in general, have been outlined. I hope that this study, and others like it, will be instrumental in helping planners as well as older persons to avoid the building of a "false paradise."

References

Becker, Howard S., "Personal Change in Adult Life," *Sociometry*, March 1964, 40–53.

Birren, James E., "Principles of Research on Aging," in *Handbook of Aging and the Individual*, James E. Birren, Ed., Chicago: University of Chicago Press, 1959, pp. 3–42.

Cumming, Elaine, and Henry, William H., *Growing Old: The Process of Disengagement*, New York: Basic Books, 1961.

Emerson, Joan P., "Nothing Unusual is Happening," Paper read at Annual Meeting of the American Sociological Association, September 1969.

Goffman, Erving, *Asylums*. Garden City, N.Y.: Doubleday, 1961, pp. 1–124.

Goffman, Erving, "On Cooling the Mark Out," *Psychiatry* 15, 451–463, November 1952.

Kuhlen, Raymond G., "Developmental Changes in Motivation During the Adult Years," in *Middle Age and Aging*, Bernice L. Neugarten, Ed., Chicago: University of Chicago Press, 1968, pp. 115–136.

Maullin, Richard, "Los Angeles Liberalism," *Trans-Action*, 8 (7), 41, May 1971.

Miller, Stephen J., "The Social Dilemma of the Aging Leisure Participant," in *Older People and Their World: The Subculture of Aging*, Arnold M. Rose and Warren A. Peterson, Eds., Philadelphia: F. A. Davis, 1965, pp. 77–92.

New York Times, The, September 21, 1972, p. 39.

Rose, Arnold M., "The Subculture of the Aging: A Topic for Sociological Research," *Gerontologist*, 2: 123–127.

Rose, Arnold M., "A Current Theoretical Issue in Social Gerontology," *Gerontologist*, 4: 46–50.

Simmel, George, "The Metropolis and Mental Life," in *Contemporary Society*, ed. by the staff, Chicago: University of Chicago Book Store, 1942, Ch. IX, pp. 1–18.

Streib, Gordon F., "Are the Aged a Minority Group?" in *Applied Sociology*, Alvin W. Gouldner and Warren A. Peterson, Eds., New York: Free Press, 1965, pp. 311–328.

Weber, Max, *The Protestant Ethic and the Spirit of Capitalism*, New York: Charles Scribner's Sons, 1958.

Wilensky, Harold L., "Work, Careers and Social Integration," *International Social Science Journal*, 12, pp. 543–560, 1960.

Recommended readings

Becker, Howard, and Strauss, Anselm, "Careers, Personality, and Adult Socialization," *American Journal of Sociology*, 62: 253–263, 1956.

Cumming, Elaine, and Henry, W., *Growing Old: The Process of Disengagement.* New York: Basic Books, 1961.

Eisenstadt, S. N., *From Generation to Generation: Age Groups and Social Structure.* Glencoe, Ill.: Free Press, 1956.

Fulton, Robert, Ed., *Death and Identity.* New York: John Wiley, 1956.

Glaser, Barney, and Strauss, Anselm, "Temporal Aspects of Dying as a Non-Scheduled Status Passage," *American Journal of Sociology*, 71, No. 1, 1965.

Glaser, Barney, and Strauss, Anselm, *Awareness of Dying.* Chicago: Aldine, 1965.

Hughes, Everett C., *Men and Their Work.* Glencoe, Ill.: Free Press, 1958, Ch. 3.

Kalish, R. A., "The Aged and the Dying Process: The Inevitable Decisions," *Journal of Social Issues*, 21 (4): 87–96, 1965.

Litwak, E., "Occupational Mobility and Extended Family Cohesion," *American Sociological Review*, 25: 385–394, 1960.

Lowenthal, Marjorie F., *Lives in Distress: The Paths of the Elderly to the Psychiatric Ward.* New York: Basic Books, 1964.

Maddox, George L., "Retirement as a Social Event in the U.S." in *Aging and Social Policy*, J. McKenney and F. T. de Vyver, Eds., New York: Appleton-Century-Crofts, 1966, pp. 119–135.

Maddox, George L., "Disengagement Theory: A Critical Evaluation," *Gerontologist,* 4, pp. 80–83, 1964.

Neugarten, Bernice, "Adult Personality: Toward a Psychology of the Life Cycle" in *Middle Age and Aging*, Bernice L. Neugarten, Ed., Chicago: University of Chicago Press, 1968.

Neugarten, Bernice, and Moore, Joan W., "The Changing Age Status System," in *Middle Age and Aging*, Bernice L. Neugarten, Ed., Chicago: University of Chicago Press, 1968.

Nosow, Sigmund, and Form, William, Eds., "The Meaning of Work," in *Man, Work, and Society.* New York: Basic Books, 1962, Ch. 2.

Parsons, Talcott, "Age and Sex in the Social Structure of the U.S.," *American Sociological Review*, 7: 604–620, 1942.

Riley, Matilda, and Foner, Anne, *Aging and Society*, Vol. 1. New York: Russell Sage Foundation, 1968.

Rose, Arnold M., "The Sub-Culture of the Aging: A Topic for Sociological Research," *Gerontologist*, 2: 123–127, 1962.

Rose, Arnold M., "A Current Theoretical Issue in Social Gerontology," *Gerontologist,* 4: 46–50, 1965.

Rosenmayer, Leopold, and Kockeis, Eva, "Propositions for a Sociological Theory of Aging and the Family," *International Social Sciences Journal*, 15: (3), 410–426, 1963.

Streib, Gordon, "Are the Aged a Minority Group?," in *Applied Sociology,* A. W. Gouldner and S. M. Miller, Eds., New York: Free Press, 1965, Ch. 24.

Sudnow, David, *Passing on: The Social Organization of Dying.* Englewood Cliffs, N.J.: Prentice-Hall, 1968.

Videbeck, Richard, and Knox, Alan B., "Alternative Participatory Responses to Aging," in *Older People and Their Social World*, A. M. Rose and W. A. Peterson, Eds., Philadelphia: F. A. Davis, 1965, pp. 37–48.

For a more comprehensive reading list on aging see references at the end of *Middle Age and Aging*, Bernice L. Neugarten, Ed. Chicago, Ill.: University of Chicago Press, (1968).